- 2

CHILLERS 5

A Shock for Ann by Sandra Woodcock

Wheel of Fortune by Iris Howden

Published in association with the Adult Literacy
and Basic Skills Unit

Hodder & Stoughton

A MEMBER OF THE HODDER HEADLINE GROUP

The publishers and ALBSU wish to acknowledge the contribution of the NEWMAT
Project, Nottinghamshire Local Education Authority, and of the Project Leader,
Peter Beynon, in the conception, writing and publication of the *Chillers* series.

British Library Cataloguing in Publication Data

Woodcock, Sandra
  A shock for Ann. – (Chillers: 5)
  1. English language – Readers
  I. Title   II. Howden, Iris   III. National Institute of Adult Education (England
  and Wales). *Adult Literacy and Basic Skills Unit*   IV. Series
  428.6

  ISBN 0-340-52106-6

First published 1989
Impression number 10 9 8 7 6 5
Year   1998   1997   1996   1995

Typeset by Gecko Limited, Bicester, Oxon
Printed in Great Britain for Hodder & Stoughton Educational, a division of
Hodder Headline Plc, 338 Euston Road, London NW1 3BH
by Redwood Books, Trowbridge, Wiltshire.

A Shock for Ann

Ann is going to die tonight.
I know because I've fixed it.
What makes a man want to kill his own wife?
It's another man of course –
the oldest reason in the book.
I can't ignore it and I won't divorce her,
so this is the best way.

It's been going on too long.
Every Wednesday night – my darts night –
she's with him.
'There's nothing in it, Peter,' she says.
'Bobby's nothing to me – not in the way you think.'
She must think I'm daft.
I've seen her looking at him.
She never looks at me like that.
She even dreams about him,
talks in her sleep.

I must admit I'm jealous,
angry too.
After all I'm a good husband.
I'm not bad looking.
Why should she make a fool of herself
over another man?
It makes her look cheap.
That's how I see it anyway.

When she can't see him she's thinking about him
or writing to him.
She thinks I don't know.
Only yesterday I heard her on the phone,
talking to her friend, Jackie,
going on about *him*.
She didn't know I'd come into the kitchen,
didn't know I was listening to her,
giggling like a silly teenager.

It was then that I made up my mind.
I'd had enough.
I'm not playing second fiddle to any man.
So I planned it –
worked on the electrics
while she was at her mother's last night.

Perfect! She can die looking at him.
When she switches on tonight for her *Dallas* fix
she'll get a shock!
That Bobby Ewing – his face comes on
right at the beginning.
I've timed it for then.
I can't wait till it's all over
so I can throw out
all the photos and scrapbooks she's collected.
Clear out all her videos.
I'll just sit here and finish my pint,
wait for the news.

Wheel of Fortune

Paul shut the door behind him with a bang.
He picked up his fishing gear
and set off for the canal.
It was time for some peace and quiet.
Brenda hadn't stopped nagging him all week.
He thought back to last Saturday.
They'd set off for the T.V. studios
in such a good mood.
It was all going to be a laugh –
a bit of fun.

It was Brenda's idea about the quiz show,
Wheel of Fortune.
'You'd be good on it,' she said.
'You always know the answers.'
So he wrote in.
He got a letter back after four weeks.
He was going to be on it –
a live T.V. show!
He found out that it wasn't so easy.
It was hot under the studio lights.
The game moved so fast –
it was a race between him and two others.

One of them, the woman, was quick.
Her finger was always first on the buzzer.
The other one, an older man, was slow –
but he knew a lot.
Paul had his work cut out to stay in the game.

Half-way through,
one of them would have to drop out.
Then the game would go on with just two players.
The questions would be worth more money.
At the end of the show
only one person would be left
to spin the Wheel of Fortune –
maybe to win a really big prize
or maybe to lose the lot.
That was what made it so good to watch.

'Just take the money if you win,' Brenda told him.
'You could lose the lot if you spin the wheel.'
But when he'd got through to the end,
and the quiz-master led him
to the front of the stage,
he couldn't make up his mind.
'Spin the wheel! Spin the wheel!'
the crowd shouted.

The quiz-master put his arm
around Paul's shoulder.
He read out some of the prizes he might win –
a washing machine, a gold watch,
a set of china dishes and lots more.
Some of the slots on the wheel were blank.
These were the mystery prizes.
You might win a holiday or lose the lot
and just get a booby prize –
like a box of matches.

The quiz-master kept talking all the time.
Paul didn't know what to do.
He looked into the audience.
Beyond the stage it was dark.
He couldn't see where Brenda was sitting.
'What should he do, ladies and gentlemen?'
the quiz-master asked.
'Spin the wheel! Spin the wheel!'
they shouted again.
Paul nodded.

The quiz-master spun the wheel.
It whizzed round at speed.
Then it slowed down
and the silver hand in the middle
pointed first at one number then at another.
At last it stopped at number 18.
The quiz-master took an envelope
out of the number 18 slot.
He began to open it very very slowly.
Paul wished he would get on with it.
'You have won . . .,' he said,
'the chance to come back on our "Winners" Show.
There'll be big prizes to be won.
Do you want to take the £275 you have won tonight
or will you come back?'
'Come back! Come back!' the crowd yelled.
'I'll come back,' Paul said at last.

11

'You fool,' Brenda said.
'Think what we could have done with £275.
You go and risk the lot.
It's a pity you didn't win a useful prize
like a washing machine.'
'Oh shut it, Brenda,' Paul said.
'I'm going fishing.'

He spread his gear out on the bank.
He set up the keep net and stood back
to make a cast.
Just then a man came along the tow path.
Paul waited for him to pass,
but the man stopped and spoke.
'Didn't I see you on T.V. last night?' he asked.
Paul put down his rod. He nodded.
'You did well,' the man said,
'going for the big prizes.'
'Yes,' said Paul, 'but I'm not sure that I'm doing
the right thing.
My wife thinks I'm mad.'
'Well, the questions do get harder as you go on,'
the man said.
'That's what Brenda says.
It's beginning to worry me a bit.'

'There are ways and means,' the man said
with a strange look.
'How do you mean?' Paul asked.
'I could find out the questions they'll be using,'
the man said.
Paul looked at him.
He seemed to be quite serious.
'Think about it,' the man said.
'If you want my help give me a ring.'
He wrote a phone number on a scrap of paper
and gave it to Paul.

He began to walk away,
but then he turned back to Paul.
'There's just one thing,' he said.
'What's that?'
'It'll cost you.
If you take my help, I'll expect a favour in return.'

He gave Paul an odd smile.
Then he was gone.
He'd vanished into thin air.
'What a funny looking bloke,' Paul thought.
'So thin and dark, with that little black beard.'
Paul shook his head. 'Must be some nutter.'

It began to rain.
Paul was glad of the excuse to pack up.
His bad mood had gone.
He wanted to get home
and make it up with Brenda.

The 'Winners' Show was in three weeks.
Paul began to worry.
He spent all his time indoors
reading through quiz-books.
He tried to learn more and more facts
from the encyclopaedia.

He kept asking Brenda to test him.
'This is getting to be a drag,' she said.
'It's not a matter of life and death, Paul.
It's only a game.'
Yet Paul found it hard to sleep.
When he went to bed
his head was full of questions and answers.
He tossed and turned all night.
Then he had a strange dream.
He dreamed he had won a car on the quiz show.
He was driving it away.
But there was someone else in the car –
the strange man with the beard.

When he woke up
he thought the dream must mean something.
He looked for the phone number
that the man had given him.
When Brenda was out at the laundrette
he rang him up.

'I'll meet you by the canal bridge
at six o'clock tomorrow night,' the man told him.
'I'll have something for you.'

When Paul got to the bridge
the man seemed to come from nowhere.
He handed Paul a brown envelope.
It was sealed up.
'The answers are inside,' he said.
'You'll be all right.
But don't forget – you'll owe me a favour.'
He smiled at Paul –
the same smile as before.
There was something not quite right
about that smile –
something evil.

On the night of the show Paul felt very calm.
He took his seat
and shook hands with the other players –
a teacher and a traffic warden.
The questions began.
As the quiz-master held up card after card
Paul found he knew the answer
almost as soon as he spoke.
By half-time he was well in the lead.

The traffic warden dropped out,
and Paul was left to face the teacher.
Again, he seemed to know every answer.
Soon it was all over.
Paul had won £1,000.
But could he win the car?

The quiz-master took his hand.
He led Paul to the front of the stage.
This time Paul didn't need the crowd
to tell him what to do.
'Spin the wheel,' he said quietly.

The lights went down.
The wheel began to move faster and faster.
Paul's eyes followed it round and round
until he became dizzy.
Pictures seemed to be coming
from the middle of the wheel.
It was like the wheel of a car going very fast.

Then in the middle
he saw the face of the man with the beard.
He saw again that evil smile.
Paul's heart was fit to burst.
He could hardly breathe
and he felt a terrible pain in his chest.
Suddenly he knew that if he won the car
he would die.

Then the wheel slowed down.
The pictures faded.
The lights came back on.
The hand swung down
and came to rest at number 7.
Paul felt sick.

'Well, ladies and gentlemen,
what will our young friend take home tonight?
Will it be the sports car?
Or will it be another star prize?
Lucky 7 . . . let's see!'
The quiz-master took the envelope out of the slot.
'You have won . . .'
Paul held his breath.

'. . . a packet of extra strong mints.'
The crowd gasped – a booby prize.

Going home on the bus, Brenda didn't say a word.
Paul knew she was upset
but he just felt free –
as free as air.
No more worry,
no more racking his brains,
no more sleepless nights,
and no favours owed to that strange man.
Paul felt inside his jacket pocket
and took out the brown envelope.
It was still sealed.
At least he'd won without cheating.
He'd done it on his own.
He tore the envelope into little pieces.
Then he began to laugh.

Brenda looked at him.
'What's so funny?' she said.
'You throw away £1,000 and it's a joke?'

Paul put his arm around her and pulled her close.
'It's just like you said, Brenda.
It isn't a matter of life and death.
It's only a game.
Have an extra strong mint.'

The British Citizenship Test

FOR

DUMMIES®

by Julian Knight

The British Citizenship Test For Dummies®
Published by
John Wiley & Sons, Ltd
The Atrium
Southern Gate
Chichester
West Sussex
PO19 8SQ
England

E-mail (for orders and customer service enquires): cs-books@wiley.co.uk

Visit our Home Page on www.wiley.com

Copyright © 2006 John Wiley & Sons, Ltd, Chichester, West Sussex, England

Published by John Wiley & Sons, Ltd, Chichester, West Sussex

WILEY

About the Author

Julian Knight was born in 1972 in Chester. He was educated at the Chester Catholic High School and later Hull University, where he obtained a degree in History.

Since 2002 Julian has been the BBC News personal finance and consumer affairs reporter and has won many awards for his journalism. Previous to this, he worked for *Moneywise* magazine and wrote for the *Guardian* amongst many other publications. He has also authored *Wills, Probate, and Inheritance Tax For Dummies, Retiring Wealthy For Dummies,* and *Cricket For Dummies*.

Publisher's Acknowledgements

We're proud of this book; please send us your comments through our Dummies online registration form located at www.dummies.com/register/.

Some of the people who helped bring this book to market include the following:

Acquisitions, Editorial, and Media Development

Executive Project Editor: Martin Tribe

Development Editor: Rachael Chilvers

Executive Editor: Jason Dunne

Proofreader: Anne O'Rorke

Cover Photo: JupiterImages

Special Help: Daniel Mersey

Composition Services

Project Coordinator: Kristie Rees

Layout and Graphics: Denny Hager, Stephanie D. Jumper

Proofreader: Susan Moritz

Indexer: Stephen Ingle

Publishing and Editorial for Consumer Dummies

Diane Graves Steele, Vice President and Publisher, Consumer Dummies

Joyce Pepple, Acquisitions Director, Consumer Dummies

Kristin A. Cocks, Product Development Director, Consumer Dummies

Michael Spring, Vice President and Publisher, Travel

Kelly Regan, Editorial Director, Travel

Publishing for Technology Dummies

Andy Cummings, Vice President and Publisher, Dummies Technology/ General User

Composition Services

Gerry Fahey, Vice President of Production Services

Debbie Stailey, Director of Composition Services

Contents at a Glance

Table of Contents

Appendix B: Sample Questions and Answers for the Life in the UK Test *135*

Introduction

●●●

*B*eing British has been described as winning first
prize in the lottery of life! And the 100,000 people
who become British citizens each year couldn't agree
more. This book is for you as a would-be citizen and wel-
come visitor to these shores.

Britain is a dynamic country, rich, and diverse. It is a big
hitter in the world with a first-rate education system and
cultural heritage to die for – although the less said about
the weather and some of the cuisine, the better! No
doubt, though, if you've picked up this book, you're
already aware of a few of the benefits of coming to live
and work in Britain, and ultimately to become a citizen.

Becoming a British citizen means enjoying full voting
rights and access to all sorts of benefits as well as the
right to carry a British passport. See Part VI for more on
the rights and responsibilities of citizenship.

You'll find other books in the *For Dummies* series useful
too; check out *British History For Dummies* (Wiley) as a
useful research source for taking and passing the citizenship test.

About This Book

This book is about making your immigration and citizenship dreams a reality. In plain English, I help you jump
the administrative hurdles and cross that citizenship and
immigration finishing line.

I outline all you need to know to get into the UK, stay in the UK – either temporarily or permanently – and ultimately apply for British citizenship.

In a nutshell, here are the steps to citizenship covered in this book:

- ✔ **Getting into and staying in the UK.** Initially you can enter the UK by getting a visa and a work permit. If you want to extend your stay you have to fill out the right immigration forms in order to be granted *leave to remain* or *right of abode* (see Part I for more on what these mean).

- ✔ **Taking and passing the citizenship test.** After you've lived in the UK for long enough – usually five years – you can apply for citizenship. First you must take and pass the citizenship test (the *Life in the UK* test), or prove your English skills and knowledge of UK life by taking a course at a college of further education.

- ✔ **Attending the citizenship ceremony.** You take the oath of allegiance at the citizen ceremony. This is the proud moment when you officially become a British citizen.

Conventions Used in This Book

Immigration to the UK can be tricky, with lots of paperwork and fiendishly complex rules to understand, as well as a fair smattering of jargon.

Have no fears – the main aim of this book is to junk the jargon, and explain immigration and citizenship rules and the paperwork with crystal-clear clarity. I put new terms in *italics* and always follow them with an explanation. Web addresses appear in `monofont`.

As you look through this book you'll see text in grey boxes. The information in these sidebars is interesting (I hope) but not essential to your understanding of the subject matter. So when you see a sidebar, the choice is yours: you can either read it or not. No sweat if you decide to skip the sidebars – you won't be missing out on absolutely vital information.

Foolish Assumptions

In writing this book I make the assumption that you're not an expert in immigration or gaining citizenship.

I also assume you're willing to put in the hard work! If you're going to reach your immigration and citizenship goals, you're going to have to show patience and take on the paperwork. The good news is that this book gives you the lowdown on all the paperwork you'll come across and points out relevant sources of help.

How This Book Is Organised

This book has seven main parts and two appendixes. Each part looks at a different aspect of UK immigration from coming to the UK for a short stay to taking the citizenship test, all the way through to the rights you enjoy when you become a British citizen.

Part 1: Deciding to Stay in the UK

This part covers getting into the UK by applying for a visa in your country of origin, and what can happen at immigration in UK airports and seaports. This part also explains what to do if you're seeking asylum. Perhaps most importantly, this gives you the heads-up on the requirements you need to apply for citizenship.

Part II: Getting to Know the Immigration and Citizenship Players

Part II gives you an overview of all the players in the immigration and citizenship game. This part covers key government agencies, the main charities that can offer aid, and legal help you can get.

Part III: Taking Care of Immigration and Citizenship Paperwork

This part unravels the mysteries of the myriad forms and paperwork involved in immigration and citizenship. Occasionally, you may be called for an interview with the authorities during the process, so read this part for how to deal with the interview process.

Part IV: Taking the Citizenship Test

The clue is in the title. Part IV explains the preparation you need to do to take the test, and how to book and sit a test. If you pass the test – congratulations! – this part also describes the citizenship ceremony where you celebrate your new status as a British citizen.

If your spoken English isn't very developed, this part also explains a bit about taking a course to improve your communication skills.

Part V: Troubleshooting Your Application

With all the paperwork and departments involved, it's no surprise that things can and do go wrong occasionally. This part prepares you for potential problems with your application – forewarned is forearmed.

Part V also warns you about the waiting times involved in your application – you need a big dose of patience to play this citizenship game!

Part VI: Reaping the Rewards of Citizenship

From a brand-new British passport enabling you to travel freely in the European Union, through to free healthcare and education, being a British citizen brings a wealth of benefits. This part explains those benefits – and the responsibilities that come with them.

Part VII: Ten Helpful For Dummies Books

This chapter lists ten useful *For Dummies* books that you may want to get hold of to help you integrate into life in the UK. From helping you figure out how to buy and sell a home in Britain through to the complexities of the very British sport of cricket, this little list will have you enlightened and amused.

Appendix A

This appendix consists of the chapters from the Home Office's *Life in the United Kingdom: A Journey to Citizenship* on which the Life in the UK test is based. The chapters cover British history, festivals, and politics, as well as a fair few facts and figures about the population. You need to study this appendix carefully, as all the questions in the test are based on this information.

Appendix B

This appendix has nearly 200 sample questions to start testing yourself with in preparation for the Life in the UK test. This appendix also has all the answers to the questions – no cheating, now! Study Appendix A, get the sample questions right in Appendix B, and you'll be well equipped to pass the citizenship test with flying colours.

Icons Used in This Book

The small graphics in the margins of this book point to parts of the text that you may want to pay special attention to.

The information marked by this bull's-eye highlights helpful strategies you'd be wise to follow.

Bear in mind the information this icon highlights to make crossing the citizenship finish line as simple as possible.

This icon highlights potential pitfalls on the road to British immigration and citizenship.

I sometimes go into a bit more detail about an issue raised in the text. You can skip these paragraphs if you don't want so much information.

Where to Go from Here

This book aims to help you navigate the UK's immigration and citizenship rules. You can read this book from cover to cover if you want to, or simply zero in on the information you need right now by using the table of contents and the index.

You may want to make notes as you go along – feel free to jot down comments in the margins of this book.

You may feel the need to get professional help achieving your immigration or citizenship ambitions. No problem, head to Part II, which is dedicated to giving you all the points of contact you need.

Part I

Deciding to Stay in the UK

In This Part

▶ Wrestling with visas

▶ Working and studying in the UK

▶ Seeking asylum

▶ Making the leap to citizenship

A s a future British citizen, perhaps you've come to the United Kingdom to find work, study, marry, or even just to take in the sights. You like what you see and experience here – apart from the notorious British weather, no doubt!

Perhaps you lay down roots, master the language, observe and appreciate the idiosyncrasies of British life such as queuing at any opportunity and wearing socks with sandals.

The logical progression is to go the whole hog and apply for *British citizenship,* a qualification that enables you to play a full part in the social, political, and economic life of your new adopted home.

In this part, I take you through an overview of the journey from holidaymaker, visiting student, or worker to fully fledged British citizen.

Plotting Your Path to Citizenship

Over 100,000 people become British citizens each year. Both the number of people coming from abroad to live in the UK and applicants for British citizenship have risen sharply in recent years.

You can sum up the usual path to citizenship as:

1. Get into the UK through visas and work permits.

2. Stay in the UK by being granted *leave to remain* or *right of abode* (see later in this part for more on these).

3. Apply for citizenship by living in the UK for long enough and passing the citizenship test.

Looking at Why People Come to the UK

Your first taste of Britain, apart from films starring Hugh Grant and novels by Jane Austen, was probably by:

- **Coming here on a holiday.** Britain loves tourists and is proud of its unique history and heritage.

- **Coming here to work.** With a shortage of labour, Britain welcomes workers from abroad. The British economy is a star performer compared to many of its European rivals, with plenty of relatively well-paid jobs. Unsurprisingly, Britain attracts large numbers of people, particularly from poorer Eastern European countries.

✔ **Coming here to study.** The UK is famed for its educational institutions. English is the world's premier language of business and the media, so it's no surprise that the UK is a magnet for foreign students.

Perhaps you came to the UK for more personal reasons such as marriage, or you're simply exercising your birthright to live in Britain.

The main reasons for people coming to Britain either for a short or permanent stay are:

✔ Tourism

✔ Employment

✔ Education

✔ Marriage

✔ Birthright

Britain has a complex and multilayered immigration system in place to deal with every scenario.

Getting to Grips with the Visa System

When travelling to the UK, the first question you need to ask yourself is 'Do I need a visa for my visit?'

Do I need a visa?

A *visa* is a document telling immigration officials at airports and seaports why you're coming to the UK and how long you're allowed to stay. The visa certificate is put in your passport or travel document by an immigration official (an *Entry Clearance Officer* or ECO) at a British Embassy, Consulate, or High Commission in your country of origin. The visa gives you permission to enter the UK.

Not everyone needs a visa to visit Britain. People from some countries can come here on holiday without a visa but cannot study or work in the UK without one. Check with your local British Embassy, Consulate, or High Commission in your country of origin. You can find your local Embassy, Consulate, or High Commission at www.embassiesabroad.com. You can also take a look at the UK visa Web site at www.ukvisas.gov.uk for more details. You can apply for a visa by post, in person, or online.

You can obtain a visa in your country of origin from a British Embassy, Consulate, or High Commission. You're charged a fee for the visa in the local currency. Part III has more details about the different types of visas you can apply for to stay or work in Britain.

If you require a visa to visit the UK on holiday or to visit family, the Entry Clearance Officer in the Embassy, Consulate, or High Commission of your native country needs to see evidence that you intend to return. Take your return-flight booking details as evidence that you intend to return to your native country.

Attending a visa interview

Your application for a UK visa may be approved by the ECO in the Embassy, Consulate, or High Commission in your country of origin based purely on the application form. Sometimes, though, the immigration control ask you to attend a short interview.

The majority of these interviews are merely routine and are carried out in a public office at the Embassy, Consulate, or High Commission in your country of origin. However, if you need a visa for the purpose of marriage – where you have married or plan to marry a British national – then the interview is carried out in a private room to respect your privacy during questioning.

The ECO may want to ask you specific questions about your trip. For example, if you're studying, the ECO may want to assess whether you can support yourself while studying without recourse to working illegally (working without a working visa).

Your visa application is dealt with by an Entry Clearance Office (ECO). The Entry Clearance Manager (ECM) supervises ECOs. If you're unhappy with how the ECO deals with your case, you can complain immediately to the ECM.

Working in the UK

The UK needs workers, both skilled and unskilled, to fuel its growing economy. The UK's immigration authority want to ensure that those coming to the UK contribute to, rather than drain, resources.

When deciding whether to allow you into the UK in the first place, or extend your stay temporarily or permanently, the immigration authorities make a judgement on your usefulness to Britain. Being highly skilled and educated and already having a steady job or offer of work are all factors that count in your favour.

Workers from the European Union

If you're from the European Economic Area (EEA) or European Union (EU), you're free to come to the UK and work. You can also bring your spouse and children along, who can also work or go to school, as long as they too are EEA/EU nationals. If your family members are not EEA/EU nationals, they'll need a visa and may not be able to work.

The citizens of 28 countries are defined as EEA/EU nationals. You can find the full list of countries on the IND Web site at www.ind.homeoffice.gov.uk/applying/eeaeu nationals. EU countries include France, Germany, and Ireland as well as nations that joined in 2004 such as Poland, Hungary, Lithuania, and Estonia.

People from the new member states (that joined in 2004) must register with the Home Office before starting work. Getting registered is a formality. To get a Worker Registration Scheme application form (form EEA1), call 08705 210 224. The form EEA1 is very simple. You're asked for your name, address, date of birth, nationality, and employment details.

After you've worked legally in the UK for 12 consecutive months, you have full rights of free movement and no longer need to register on the Worker Registration Scheme.

Workers from outside the European Union

Work permits are issued by Work Permits UK, part of the Home Office's *Immigration and Nationality Directorate* (IND) scheme (Part II has more about the IND). The IND scheme enables UK employers to recruit people from outside the European Economic Area or European Union. Work permits also allow people from overseas to come to the UK for training or work experience.

Your would-be UK employer must apply for a UK work permit for you – you cannot apply yourself. Your potential employer needs to contact Work Permits UK at least eight weeks before the date you need to start work. Check out the Government's Web site `www.workingin theuk.gov.uk` for more information about work permits.

The five types of work permit are:

- ✔ **Business and commercial permits:** Enable UK firms to employ workers from abroad to fill vacancies that they can't fill with British citizens.

- ✔ **Internships:** Allow students from abroad to come to the UK on an *internship* (period of training) with an employer in the UK, usually as part of a course of study.

- ✔ **Training and work experience schemes:** Enable people from abroad to come to the UK to undertake work-based training for either a qualification or simply work experience.

✔ **Sportspeople and entertainers:** Can come to the UK to ply their trade. You usually need a work permit, but if you're coming to do personal appearances, you could come as a business visitor in which case you don't need a permit. You also don't need a work permit if you have an invitation to perform at one or more specific events (such as concert venues or festivals). You may need a visa to get into the UK though.

✔ **Food-manufacturing industry schemes:** Allow people from abroad to come to the UK for up to 12 months to take up low-skilled work in the food manufacturing industry.

Although many work permit arrangements last a year or more, the idea is that you fulfil your contract of employment and then return to your country of origin.

If you come to the UK under work permit rules, your spouse and dependents can join you. However, your family has to apply for a visa at the local British Embassy, Consulate, or High Commission in their country of origin.

Fast-tracking your way to a work permit

Special immigration rules relate to particular groups of workers such as au pairs, health service workers, and film workers. The big idea is to allow easy entry into the UK for people with much-needed skills. For the inside track on how the rules affect particular groups of workers check out www.workingintheuk.gov.uk.

To find out more about issues such as whether you'll be taxed, whether you'll be paid sick leave, or whether you'll have the option to contribute to a pension scheme while you work in the UK, visit www.workingintheuk.org.uk.

Turning a Flying Visit into a Longer Stay

So you come to the UK, decide you love the place, and can't bear to leave. You have two options when applying to stay for longer:

- ✔ You can return to your country of origin and submit an application from there.
- ✔ You can make your application to remain in the UK from Britain.

Perhaps the purpose of your visit is changing – for example, you initially visit the UK as a holidaymaker but then want to remain to study. You need to return to your country of origin and apply for a new visa through your local British Embassy, Consulate, or High Commission.

However, if you're looking to extend your stay in the UK for work purposes or to get married, you can apply through the Home Office's Immigration and Nationality Directorate (IND). Head to Part II for more on this big beast of the immigration jungle.

Studying in the UK

To come to the UK to study, you must show the ECO evidence that you've been accepted on a course of study at an educational establishment approved by the UK's

Department for Education and Skills (DFES). Look at www.dfes.gov.uk/providerregister to find out whether the college where you want to study is registered.

In addition, you must be able to show that you can support yourself financially, without having to work.

Marrying a Brit: No guarantee of citizenship

Sometimes people come to the UK and marry a British citizen in the belief that they themselves will become a citizen. I'm afraid it doesn't work like that. You don't automatically acquire British citizenship through marriage. You may be allowed *leave to remain* (this means you can live in the UK for a specific period, initially two years and then a further three years) in the country following a marriage – but marriage doesn't guarantee citizenship. You have to apply for British citizenship separately if you want it.

However, marriage can be a passport – pardon the pun – to *UK residency*, the right to remain in Britain. You and your spouse will probably be interviewed by immigration as part of the UK residency process. The immigration authorities want to be sure that the marriage is genuine – rather than contrived for the purposes of allowing the non-British partner to stay in the UK – before granting leave to remain.

If you're a British citizen marrying a national of a foreign country, you don't lose your nationality. In fact, you may eventually obtain *dual nationality* – enabling you to keep all the rights of a British citizen such as the right to vote in the UK, and also the rights of your spouse's country, providing that both countries allow dual nationality. If you gain British citizenship and your country of origin does not allow dual citizenship, it may either consider you to have lost your original nationality or simply not recognise your new British nationality – how rude!

If you already have a degree, or if you want to study science or engineering, you can apply for a work permit during your studies. In addition, as a science or engineering student you can stay in the UK for up to 12 months after your studies have finished and take up work. On completing their studies, other students must leave the UK.

You need to apply to study in the UK from your country of origin through your local British Embassy, Consulate, or High Commission. See www.embassiesabroad.com to find your local embassy.

Living in the UK: The right of abode

The *right of abode* is the right to live and work in the UK. When granted, it means you do not have to deal with the immigration services or obtain a visa or a *right to remain* permit). The right of abode doesn't quite carry all the weight of citizenship – see Part VI for more on citizenship rights – but it comes a very close second.

You have the right of abode if:

- ✔ You were adopted as a child in the UK by a British adopter.

- ✔ You are a citizen of a *Commonwealth* country (former countries of the British Empire that are members of the Commonwealth organisation) before 31 December 1982 and one of your parents or adopters is a British citizen.

- ✔ You are a female Commonwealth citizen before 31 December 1982 and are, or were, married to a man with the right of abode in the UK.

Overstaying your welcome

On expiration of your visa, you're expected to leave Britain in double-quick time. Even a delay of just a few days can cause a nasty scene with immigration and make returning to the UK difficult in the future.

The sanctions taken against people who overstay in Britain can be severe. Overstaying on a visa is a criminal offence and can lead to detention, prosecution, a fine, or imprisonment. In addition, you are deported from the UK and are unlikely to ever be allowed back in.

You can apply for a right of abode *certificate of entitlement* from the UK Home Office at: Home Office Nationality Group (Right of Abode), PO Box 306, Liverpool, L2 7XS. You can also visit www.ukvisas.gov.uk. You get a gummed sticker placed in your passport, called a *certificate of entitlement*. This shows immigration officials that you can move freely into and out of the UK.

Seeking Asylum

Each year thousands of people come to the UK from abroad – often smuggled into the country – and claim asylum.

In short, *claiming asylum* means that you ask to stay in the UK because returning to your country of origin is dangerous. Asylum claims are assessed by the UK immigration service and many are unsuccessful. As an asylum seeker, you're expected to return to your country of origin when it is safer. As a result, you're only initially granted a temporary leave to remain in the UK. However, eventually, you may be granted *indefinite leave to remain* in the UK.

Ultimately, a grant of indefinite leave to remain is on a case-by-case basis. Such a grant could follow marriage to a UK citizen, or after you've been in the UK for an unspecified period of time and show you're contributing positively to the life of the country and putting down roots. Another factor that affects indefinite leave to remain is the situation of your country of origin; if you've fled a war zone, is it now safe for you to return?

Asylum seekers who satisfy all residency and citizenship test requirements (see Part IV) can apply for British citizenship.

If you have your asylum claim turned down, you're expected to return to your country of origin. Common reasons for refusal to grant asylum include:

- ✔ The immigration authorities believe that you would not be at risk if you return home.

- ✔ The authorities doubt whether you are who you say you are or come from where you say you do.

Asylum seekers who are refused leave to remain can appeal the decision. See Part V for more on troubleshooting immigration and citizenship applications.

Heading towards Citizenship

People entering the UK today may not realise that in a few short years they can become British citizens, if they want to.

In order to apply for citizenship you need to meet certain requirements, including:

- ✔ You have to live in the UK with your British citizen spouse or civil partner for at least three years.

- ✔ If you're not married to a British citizen, you have to have lived in the UK for at least five years. You must not have been out of the UK for more than 450 days during that time.

- ✔ You have not been out of the UK for more than 90 days during the previous year.

- ✔ You must be aged 18 or older and of sound mind.

- ✔ You must not have been living in the UK in breach of the UK immigration rules at any time.

If you tick all the above, you can apply for British citizenship. The preceding requirements are just the start: you must also pay a fee, you must be competent in written and spoken English, and you must pass the British citizenship test. Part IV has the inside track on how to obtain citizenship rights.

Gaining full British citizenship isn't simply about acquiring a natty certificate and then applying for a passport. British citizens enjoy freedoms and privileges that are the envy of many other countries. See Part VI for the rights – and responsibilities – that British citizenship brings.

You can follow one of two paths to citizenship: *naturalisation* and *registration*.

- ✔ **Naturalisation** is when you come to the UK and fulfil the requirements to become a British citizen through the length of your stay and other factors, such as being married to your British partner for three years.

✔ **Registration** is a far less frequent route to citizenship than naturalisation, open to citizens of Britain's overseas territories such as the Falkland Islands and Gibraltar. All you're doing through registration is claiming your right to British citizenship.

Part II

Getting to Know the Immigration and Citizenship Players

● ●

In This Part

▶ Checking out immigration controls

▶ Recognising the main government agencies

▶ Making the most of charitable aid

▶ Resorting to legal help

● ●

*B*efore you start your journey to British citizenship, you need to know about whom you're dealing with.

This part explains the roles of the different government agencies you'll encounter from when you first come to the UK to the time you gain citizenship. I explain how these agencies can impact your bid for immigration and citizenship.

Dealing with government agencies can be daunting, but don't worry – this part also explains all the help and advice out there for you, from charities to legal help.

Understanding Immigration Controls

All countries look to control immigration. First up, immigration is about making sure that people coming from abroad to the UK have the right skills to add to Britain's social and economic life. Immigration controls also regulate how long people from abroad can stay; what you do when you're here; whether your relatives can join you in the UK; and whether you can use the National Health Service or claim benefits.

You can break down the immigration process into two different parts:

- Pre-entry clearance to come to the UK on holiday, for work, to study, or to get married by obtaining a visa and/or a work permit.

- Permission after you're in the UK to remain temporarily or permanently through being granted *indefinite leave to remain* or British citizenship (see Part I for more about leave to remain).

The following sections explain the agencies involved in immigration and your goal of becoming a British citizen.

Meeting the Main Government Agencies

Say the word 'government' and many people think of faceless bureaucrats and professional paper pushers. Ditch the stereotype and bear in mind that government agencies are there to ensure that the law of the land is applied fairly. You have to work with and cooperate with these agencies in order to make your British citizenship dream a reality.

British Missions overseas

People from certain countries need a visa to come to the UK, even for a holiday. Whether you need to apply for a visa or not depends on your country of origin and the purpose of your trip to the UK. For example, a holiday-maker from Australia does not need a visa, but an Aussie wanting to come to the UK to work for more than six months does need one.

You need to apply for a visa in your country of origin at your local British Embassy, Consulate, or High Commission. Your visa application is scrutinised by an immigration official – called an *Entry Clearance Officer* or ECO – in the Embassy, Consulate, or Mission. You may be called for an interview to answer questions about what you plan to do while you're in the UK. Parts I and III have loads more on who needs a visa and how to obtain one.

UK visas are often initially limited to six months. If you overstay your limit imposed by your visa without permission, you can be prosecuted and deported.

Visa rules can be complex, so check out www.ukvisa.gov.uk for more details.

Work Permits UK

This agency does exactly what you'd expect, and deals with issuing work permits. If you want to come to the UK to work, you may need a work permit to do so. See Part I for more on how to obtain a work permit.

Immigration and Nationality Directorate (IND)

If you want to turn your visit into a permanent stay you have to apply to the Immigration and Nationality Directorate in the UK for permission. This organisation is a branch of the Government's Home Office (the government department responsible for internal affairs). Put simply, the IND's job is to decide who can and can't stay in the UK, whether for a couple of years to study, or on a permanent basis.

The IND's job is to:

- ✔ Assess cases of people who are claiming asylum – removing those whose applications fail and integrating successful claimants.

- ✔ Decide on whether spouses or civil partners should be allowed to stay in the UK.

- ✔ Ensure that people leave when they're no longer entitled to be in the UK, for example, when a visa expires.

- ✔ Decide on whether people can extend their stay in the UK.

- ✔ Assess and process applications for British citizenship.

As you can see, the IND has a lot on its plate! The IND employs more than 17,000 staff. It can be bureaucratic and slow to make decisions. See Part V for more on average waiting times for applications.

The British Missions – such as embassies, consulates, and High Commissions – are run by the UK Foreign and Commonwealth Office, yet the Immigration and Nationality Directorate is run by the UK Home Office. Why the difference? Simple: the British Missions deal with people based abroad, while the IND works with people after they've come to the UK.

You can find out lots more about the IND at their Web site at www.ind.homeoffice.gov.uk.

The Immigration Service

This service is a subdivision of the Immigration and Nationality Directorate and deals with the screening and detention of asylum seekers. The Immigration Service also deals with immigration control at UK airports and seaports.

Asylum and Immigration Tribunal

If your request to remain in the UK is rejected by the IND, then you may have the right to appeal the decision. The Asylum and Immigration Tribunal (AIT) is your port of call. This organisation examines your case and decides whether the UK immigration rules were applied properly in your case. AIT then decides whether you can stay or have to leave the UK. For more details on appealing an immigration or asylum decision, check out Part V or the AIT's Web site at www.ait.gov.uk.

Feeling under the weather?

Britain is one of the few countries in the world to offer free universal healthcare. The National Health Service (NHS) is the one of the biggest employers in the Western world; it treats millions of patients each year through a system of General Practitioners (GPs) and hospitals. NHS treatment is free for everyone living in the UK – not only British citizens. For more details, check out www.nhsdirect.nhs.uk.

If you're ill and need NHS treatment, you must first visit a GP (unless it's an emergency, in which case you go straight to your local hospital's Accident and Emergency unit). The GP examines you and may refer you to a specialist doctor, called a consultant, for treatment. See Part VI for more on the workings of the NHS.

Office of the Immigration Services Commissioner (OISC)

The Office of the Immigration Services Commissioner (OISC) exists to ensure that everyone gets the right immigration advice. OISC can't help with individual applications submitted to the IND or offer advice, but they can point immigrants and would-be citizens in the right direction for help. The OISC Web site at www.oisc.gov.uk gives details about how to find an immigration adviser and how to lodge a complaint if you feel you've been badly treated by the IND or another governmental body.

National Asylum Support Service (NASS)

As a new arrival to the UK, you're supposed to look after yourself financially so that you're not a drain on national resources by relying on the State to support you. However, if you are an asylum seeker, you're not allowed to work while your application to remain in the UK is being considered by the IND. This leaves you in a Catch 22 situation, particularly as you may have come to the UK with next to nothing. This is where the National Asylum Support Service steps in. Set up in 2000, the NASS allows asylum seekers access to health, education, and limited financial support – around £32 a week for a single person.

To claim help from the NASS as an asylum seeker, you have to show that you're *destitute* (with no money or resources) or likely to become destitute in the next fortnight. Your local authority can help you find adequate nighttime accommodation as long as you apply for asylum 'as soon as reasonably practicable'. In short, this usually means within a few days of arriving in the UK.

Immigration Advisory Service (IAS)

Although funded by the Home Office, the Immigration Advisory Service has a history of independence and tends to fight the corner of immigrants. The IAS offers free advice on all aspects of immigration and nationality law. In some instances they represent immigrants who have been denied permission to stay in the UK at appeal.

The IAS has offices at major airports and seaports as well as in large towns and cities. For more details on the IAS, and for online advice on immigration and nationality issues, check out their Web site at www.iasuk.org.

Casting an eye over the benefits system

The UK benefits and pensions system works on a *contributory principle*. This means that in order to claim Jobseekers Allowance or Incapacity Benefit, for example – two of the main benefits paid to the unemployed and those unable to work – you have to have paid National Insurance Contributions (NICS). Logically, if you haven't been living in the UK, then you haven't been contributing NICS, in which case you cannot receive certain benefits. For more on the UK benefits system check out the Web site of the Department of Work and Pensions at www.dwp.gov.uk.

Nationality Checking Service

Immigration and citizenship applications involve a lot of paperwork (see Part V for the lowdown on all the form-filling). The forms can be complex, particularly if English isn't your first language. Therefore, many local councils offer a *checking service* that entails:

- Looking over your application to ensure that you have filled it in correctly.

- Checking that you have submitted all relevant supporting documents.

- Checking that you have the correct fee ready to send to the UK immigration authorities for your application.

This checking service itself isn't free; your local authority levies a small administration charge.

The IND Web site contains a list of all local authorities offering a checking service. See www.ind.homeoffice. gov.uk/applying/nationality/ncs.

Calling on Charitable Aid

If you experience problems during your immigration process, you may feel as if you need more support than the agencies in the preceding section can offer you. Or perhaps you need advice that a government agency is not able to give you. Don't worry. Several charitable groups can offer help and advice with immigration and other issues relating to life in the UK.

Citizens Advice

You can find a Citizens Advice Bureau in most major UK towns and cities. These bureaux have advisers familiar with UK consumer and immigration law. Citizens Advice can advise you for free on the documentation you need to successfully apply for the right to remain in the UK, or to become a full British citizen. In addition, your adviser can talk you through what to do if the Immigration and Nationality Directorate refuses to let you live and work in the UK.

Take a look in your local *Yellow Pages* for details of your nearest Citizens Advice Bureau, or check out the organisation's Web site at www.adviceguide.org.uk.

UK Lesbian and Gay Immigration Group (UKLGIG)

The UK Lesbian and Gay Immigration Group is a support group for (you guessed it) lesbian and gay couples with immigration problems. The group offers advice on form filling and challenging IND decisions. The UKLGIG also campaigns against discrimination in immigration rules. You can call their helpline on 0207 620 6010, and visit their Web site at www.uklgig.org.uk.

Since 2005, all gay and lesbian couples that undergo a civil partnership ceremony in the UK have had the same legal rights as married heterosexual couples.

Refugee Council

The Refugee Council offers advice and support to newly arrived refugees and people seeking asylum in the UK. Refugee Council workers focus on helping new arrivals obtain the benefits and accommodation you're entitled to as well as talking you through the immigration application process.

Here are the details for the Refugee Council:

- ✔ **England:** Call 0207 346 6777 or visit www.refugee council.org.uk.
- ✔ **Wales:** Call 029 2048 9800 or visit www.welsh refugeecouncil.org.uk.
- ✔ **Scotland:** Call 0141 248 9799 or visit www.scottish refugeecouncil.org.uk.

Getting Yourself Legal Help

I hope that you never have to use the information in this section, but things don't always go as planned. The organisations I list here should be able to help to you deal with many aspects of the law.

Refugee Legal Centre (RLC)

The Refugee Legal Centre does what its name suggests. This charitable organisation focuses on refugees and asylum seekers who need legal representation. Perhaps you've been refused leave to remain and face possible deportation, or an application to bring over a loved one has been rejected.

You have to make an appointment to see an RLC adviser by phoning their advice line on 0207 780 3220. Check out their Web site www.refugee-legal-centre.org.uk for more details.

Law Centres

Law Centres are dotted around the country. Law Centres are free to use and they usually have a worker who specialises in immigration.

Law Centres operate a strict catchment-area policy. If you don't reside or work within the *catchment area* (the local area that the Law Centre covers), they may not see you – sorry!

To find out whether or not you live in the catchment area of a Law Centre, call the Law Centres' Federation helpline on 0207 387 8570. You can also visit www.lawcentres. org.uk.

Other lines of enquiry

Perhaps you find that the charities or Law Centres aren't much help to you, or maybe you aren't a refugee so can't ask the RLC for help. You can seek legal advice from a solicitor specialising in immigration law. Check out the

Immigration Law Practitioners' Association Web site at
www.ilpa.org.uk for details of local practitioners. Also
worth a look is the Community Legal Services Web site at
www.clsdirect.org.uk, which lists contact details of
immigration specialists. Be warned, though, legal services don't come cheap and immigration cases and disputes have a nasty habit of dragging on and on.

If you're on a low income or have no income at all, you
may be able to claim legal aid to fund your immigration
or asylum fight. Check out the Web site of the Legal
Services Commission at www.legalservices.gov.uk for
more details.

Part III

Taking Care of Immigration and Citizenship Paperwork

• •

In This Part

▶ Looking at visa forms

▶ Applying to extend your stay

▶ Dealing with immigration interviews

▶ Filling out the citizenship form

▶ Coughing up immigration and citizenship fees

• •

*I*n this part I explain the forms you need to fill out and the supporting information and documentation you have to provide in order to achieve your immigration and citizenship ambitions. You can find these forms at the Web site of the Home Office's Immigration and Nationality Directorate at www.ind.homeoffice.gov.uk.

Deciphering Visa Forms

A visa, also called *entry clearance,* gives you the right to enter and stay for a specified period in the UK. For many people, getting a visa is the first step on the long road to British citizenship.

You have to apply for a visa in your country of origin at a British Embassy, Consulate, or High Commission (see www. embassiesabroad.com to find your nearest Embassy). The visa tells the British immigration officer at a UK sea- or airport your purpose of travel and how long you can stay in the UK.

The usual maximum period a visa is granted for a holidaymaker is six months, although you can try to extend this (this part explains how). If you're a frequent visitor to the UK on business, for example, you can get a visa spanning one, two, or five years.

You can find several different types of visa application, which I describe below. These are just the main visa forms. You can also find forms for people such as diplomats, dependents of diplomats, and citizens of overseas British *dependencies* (countries that are effectively run by Britain). Take a look at the Web site www.ukvisas.gov.uk for more about these forms.

Non-settlement form (VAF1)

As the name suggests, the non-settlement form is the paperwork for people who want to come to the UK to visit, work, or study, but not to settle.

Settlement form (VAF2)

If you are the spouse, civil partner, or dependent of someone already living in the UK, and you want to come to the UK to live, you must fill in this form.

If you're the spouse, civil partner, or unmarried partner of a person looking to come to the UK to live, you're called the *sponsor*. As the sponsor, already living in the UK, you can help the application process along by providing documentary evidence that you can support the person planning to come to the UK financially and by providing accommodation.

Right of abode form (VAF4)

The right of abode form is for if you are a foreign national who believes that, due to marriage or birth, you have the legal right to live – or *abode* – in the UK. (See Part I for more on the right of abode.)

Ensuring your visa application is correct

The Entry Clearance Officer (ECO) at your local British Embassy, Consulate, or High Commission makes a decision on whether to issue you a visa based on the information contained in your application form.

Ensure that the following information is correct on your visa form:

- ✓ **Your personal details.** Make sure that you get your date of birth and nationality right!

- ✓ **The purpose of your visit.** You must be 100 per cent clear about why you want to visit Britain. If the ECO suspects that you have motives to travel other than the reason you've given, they may refuse a visa.

> ✔ **The dates you want to travel.** The visa is valid for the specific dates you want to travel. You can ask for the visa to be *post-dated* (for travel after the time the visa is signed) for up to three months.

The ECO often wants to interview visa applicants to double-check the information on your form and ensure that everything's shipshape. See the section 'Taking Immigration Interviews in Your Stride' later in this part for more on handling interviews.

Supplying supporting documents and information

Even if you swear on scout's honour that you're simply coming to the UK to visit your mum, the ECO may not take your word for it. You need documentary evidence to support your visa application. The documentary evidence you need to supply depends on what you say in your application. For example, if you want to study in the UK, you have to produce evidence that you can support yourself and that you won't work illegally. This evidence may be statements of current savings accounts, for example. Alternatively, if you're claiming the *right of abode,* you need to produce your birth, marriage, or adoption certificate. (Part I covers right of abode.)

In addition to such case-specific information you need to produce your passport and travel documentation. The ECO also needs a recent passport photograph (see Part VI for more on passport pictures).

You have to pay a visa fee in your local currency to the embassy. Your nearest British Embassy, Consulate, or High Commission can tell you how much the fee is.

Applying for an Extension of Stay in the UK

In most instances a visa only allows you to visit or work in the UK for a relatively short time – usually six months. If you want to start laying down roots in the UK and ultimately make it your home, you have to have your stay extended for a specified period of time or indefinitely.

The two types of *leave to remain* (the right to live in the UK) in the UK are temporary and indefinite. If you're planning to simply work in the UK and then return to your country of origin, apply for temporary leave rather than indefinite.

As you can imagine, you have to fill in more forms to apply for an extension to your stay. Instead of your local embassy, you deal with the Home Office's Immigration and Nationality Directorate (IND). (I discuss the IND in Part II.) You can find more information about the following forms at www.ind.homeoffice.gov.uk/applying/ applicationforms.

You need to apply for an extension of your stay *before* your current leave to remain has expired. Allow at least six weeks to apply to extend your leave to remain because the IND often takes a couple of weeks to make a decision. If you return to your country of origin, then you have to apply through your local embassy for fresh permission to return to the UK.

Applying for a temporary extension

The following sections give you the lowdown on the forms you need to apply for a temporary extension to your stay in the UK.

Getting hitched in old Blighty

If you are a foreign national with limited leave to remain, you need to fill out the nattily titled *Form COA marriage or civil partnership certificate of approval* to obtain permission to marry or register a civil partnership in the UK. However, approval of this application does not give you leave to remain in the UK.

Form FLR (M)

This application form is for an extension of stay in the UK if you are the spouse or unmarried partner of a person permanently living in the UK.

Form FLR (O)

You need to fill in this form if you want to extend your stay in the UK and you are

- A visitor undergoing medical treatment
- Working as an au pair, journalist, or language teacher
- An employee of an overseas government or airline
- A missionary
- A writer, composer, or artist
- A qualified nurse
- A person with a British grandparent

Form FLR (S)

You need this form to obtain leave to remain in the UK if you are a student or student nurse looking to resit an examination or write up an academic thesis.

Form FLR (SEGS)

If you are a science or engineering graduate, this form enables you to remain in the UK for 12 months after your studies have finished to find work.

Applying for indefinite leave to remain

Not surprisingly, _indefinite leave to remain_ allows you to stay in the UK for as long as you want. This permit is a step up from obtaining your initial visa or extending your stay in the UK.

Surprise, surprise – you have the choice of a variety of forms to fill in.

Many local authorities in the UK offer an application checking service. Staff can look over your immigration application to ensure that you've filled it in correctly and that you've submitted all relevant supporting documents along with the fee to the UK immigration authorities. See Part II for more details.

You need to make any application to extend your leave in the UK or obtain indefinite leave to remain before your existing permission to stay in the UK runs out.

Form SET (O)

Put simply, this form is for the same groups of people who would fill out Form FLR (O) (see preceding section) with a couple of additions:

- ✔ Highly skilled migrants and work permit holders
- ✔ Non-British citizens whose relationship in the UK has broken down due to domestic violence
- ✔ People with long residence in the UK

Form SET (F)

Form SET (F) is for your family members if you live permanently in the UK. Birth or adopted children under 18, parents, grandparents, or other dependent relatives need to complete this form.

Form Set (M)

This is the form for you if you want to apply for indefinite leave to remain in the UK as the spouse or unmarried partner of a person who's settled here.

Form BUS

No, it's not a double-decker . . . this form covers both extension to stay in the UK and indefinite leave to remain for business people, private investors, and wealthy retired people.

Forms ELR and HPDL

These forms are for if you are an asylum seeker who was initially granted temporary leave to remain in the UK and you want to turn your stay into a permanent one.

Whether you fill in Form ELR or HPDL depends on when you first arrived in the UK.

Taking Immigration Interviews in Your Stride

At some point in your quest to enter and stay in the UK, or to gain British citizenship, you can expect to be interviewed by an Entry Clearance Officer (ECO) at a British Embassy, Consulate, or High Commission in your country of origin, or by a UK immigration officer. Some interviews are simply routine procedure, and others are specific to your case.

Here are a few examples of immigration interviews:

- ✔ **Visa application stage.** It is standard practice for ECO's to interview visa applicants.

- ✔ **On entry to the UK.** It's not uncommon for foreign nationals coming to the UK to be interviewed by immigration officials at the UK's airports or seaports.

- ✔ **Applicants for leave to remain.** You may be called for an interview if you want indefinite leave to remain.

- ✔ **On claiming asylum.** If you claim asylum in the UK, you will be extensively interviewed by immigration officers. The officers need to fact-find so that they can reach a correct decision as to whether you'll be granted asylum.

Interviews can range from a few questions at passport control to a longer interview in private. Whatever the format of your interview, here's what you need to remember:

- ✔ **Always be truthful.** Obtaining a visa or leave to remain through deception is an offence under UK immigration laws.

- ✔ **Be polite and clear.** ECOs and immigration officers make decisions based on what you say at your interview, so how you present your case is important.

- ✔ **Consider legal representation.** If your case is complex, you may wish to consider having a lawyer who is knowledgeable about immigration law attend the interview. Refer to Part II for more on getting legal help.

When you arrive in the UK, make sure that you carry all your relevant documentation in your hand luggage in case an immigration officer wants to ask you questions.

Navigating the Citizenship Application Form

The two paths to citizenship are through naturalisation (another word for citizenship) and registration (both explained in Part I). When you apply for British citizenship via naturalisation (the most common way), the main form you need is *AN Application for Naturalisation*. You also need to take and pass the British citizenship test or gain a qualification in English and citizenship from a UK college before filling out the form. See Part IV for more.

Some of the things you're asked on the form are

- ✔ Your personal details such as your age and occupation
- ✔ Details of any solicitor who is representing you in your application
- ✔ The results of your Life in the UK test
- ✔ Your parents' date and place of birth
- ✔ Details of your marriage(s), present and past, as well as any children you have
- ✔ All addresses you've lived at in the UK during the past five years
- ✔ Precise dates for any time spent outside the UK during the past five years

✔ Character references.

✔ Details of any criminal convictions.

The form is a hefty 16 pages long and will take you a few hours to fill out properly.

If you and your spouse are both applying for British citizenship you *both* need to complete your own separate *AN Application for Naturalisation* forms.

Paying the Fees

Dealing with immigration and citizenship paperwork is a bit like being a pelican – everywhere you look you see a bill!

From getting your hands on your visa all the way through to gaining British citizenship, almost every facet of the immigration and citizenship process involves paying a fee.

The following sections tell you the typical fees you can expect to pay.

Visa fees

Expect to open your wallet for the following visa fees:

✔ **VAF1 Non-settlement:** £50 for visitors and £85 for students and workers.

✔ **VAF2 Settlement:** £260.

✔ **VAF4 Right of abode:** £85.

Visa fees are paid in local currency in your country of origin.

Extending your leave to remain and indefinite leave to remain

If you're asking for leave to remain, expect the following costs:

- ✔ **Form COA for a marriage or civil partnership:** £135.
- ✔ **Forms FLR M, O, and SEGS:** £335.
- ✔ **Form FLR S:** £250.
- ✔ **Forms SET O, F, and BUS:** £335.

Citizenship fees

Start saving your pennies for the cost of naturalisation and citizenship:

- ✔ **Individual naturalisation:** £268 (includes ceremony fee).
- ✔ **Joint naturalisation:** £336 (includes ceremony fee).
- ✔ **Registration of an adult for UK citizenship:** £188.
- ✔ **Registration of a child for UK citizenship:** £200.

Fees are likely to rise over the next few years. The Government says that by 2008 it wants to use fees to generate income to help run the UK immigration service.

Part IV

Taking the Citizenship Test

• •

In This Part

▶ Understanding the basics of the test

▶ Making the right preparations

▶ Looking at what happens post-test

▶ Perfecting your English

▶ Attending the citizenship ceremony

• •

*T*ests have an image problem. Cast your mind back to school days and tests invariably involved being stuck in a stuffy classroom on a hot day, sitting in total silence for hours on end, being watched like a hawk by the teacher in case you tried to cheat.

Fortunately, the citizenship test is not like going back to school. Sure, you need to study to take the test under exam conditions, but the whole process is lot more, well, grown-up.

In this part, I explain what the test involves and how you can go about passing it with aplomb.

Delving into the History of the Citizenship Test

The citizenship test, or Life in the UK test, was introduced by the Government in 2005. United Kingdom residents seeking British citizenship are tested to show a sufficient knowledge of the English language and of life in the UK.

The citizenship test is not designed to trip you up or weed out anyone who may not be contributing to British life. The test was introduced to ensure that, as a new-comer to Britain, you're adequately equipped for life here by encouraging you to familiarise yourself with the lan-guage, culture, and history of the British Isles.

The test makes gaining British citizenship really meaning-ful, and something to celebrate.

If you fail the citizenship test, you don't have to leave the country or have rotten tomatoes thrown at you. You can stay in the UK and retake the citizenship test. See the sec-tion 'Retaking the Test' later in this part for more advice about it.

Preparing for the Citizenship Test

All the information that you're tested on in the citizenship test is contained in the Government's study text *Life in the United Kingdom: A Journey to Citizenship.* You can buy the book from the Government's stationery office for £9.99. Check out www.tsoshop.co.uk for more details.

Or you can save your money: the crucial parts of this study text – the information you're tested upon – is reproduced in Appendix A of this book. You can find plenty of revision questions to work on in Appendix B. Read and digest the information in Appendix A, get the questions right in Appendix B, and you should have no problem passing the citizenship test.

When you take the citizenship test, you'll be quizzed on some of the following topics:

- **Society:** Including the changing role of women, migration to the UK, and the attitudes of young people.

- **Culture and diversity:** Areas covered include the population make-up of the UK – its regional and ethnic diversity – as well as national traditions and history of religious tolerance.

- **Government:** Including the roles of Parliament, the judiciary, the police, and the devolved administrations in Scotland, Wales, and Northern Ireland.

Going to College to Learn More

Further-education colleges offer courses in British citizenship. These courses focus on the Government publication *Life in the United Kingdom: A Journey to Citizenship* study text, as well as telling you more about your new country. A number of colleges combine citizenship courses with English language courses. Look in the *Yellow Pages* or your local paper to find details of your closest college. The college of your choice can send you a *prospectus* – a brochure describing all the courses on offer.

Read all about it!

You can pick a lot up about British culture, history, politics, and attitudes through newspapers, both national and locally based. Reading newspapers can also help to improve your knowledge of the English language.

You have to *either* pass the Life in the UK test *or* prove sufficient knowledge of the English language and British society by taking a combined English language and citizenship course before your application to become a British citizen will be accepted.

Charities, voluntary bodies, and some churches and mosques have trained volunteers who can help immigrants. These volunteers may not have formal language teaching skills, but they can help new immigrants integrate and get to know more about British society. This all helps in passing the citizenship test!

If you want to really get under the skin of Britain, and find out about its culture, why not brush up on its fascinating history? Lots of local colleges run courses on different aspects of British history. If you want an easy-to-understand overview, check out *British History For Dummies*.

Sitting the Test

Right – you've read the Government's *Life in the United Kingdom: A Journey to Citizenship* study text and tested yourself on the practice questions in Appendix B of this book. You're ready to take the plunge and sit the test.

Around 100 Life in the UK test centres are dotted throughout Britain. Most major UK cities and towns have a test centre. To find your nearest test centre, call the Government's Life in the UK test helpline on 0800 015 4245. Alternatively, you can visit the Life in the UK Web site at www.lifeintheuktest.gov.uk.

Demand for citizenship tests is high – you need to book an allotted time with the test centre for you to sit the test.

Here are a few things to know about sitting the test:

- ✔ Forty-five minutes are allotted for the test.
- ✔ The test is carried out online at the test centre.
- ✔ You are asked a series of 24 multiple-choice questions.
- ✔ The test fee is £34.

When you arrive at the test centre, you're taken to a computer terminal to undertake the test.

If you're not very familiar with using a computer, fear not. The Life in the UK Web site has a specially designed guide to help you get to grips with computer basics such as operating a mouse. If you are visually impaired, software is in place to enable the computer to read the test questions out loud.

Passing the test

There's no hard-and-fast pass mark for the citizenship test. The Home Office says it doesn't want to impose rigid standards. However, you're expected to get around 75 per cent of your answers correct. That equates to 18 right answers out of 24.

The test is marked online straight away. If you pass, you're given a pass notification letter at the test centre. You need this when you're applying to the Immigration and Nationality Directorate (IND) for British citizenship (see Part II for more about the IND).

If you sat a citizenship and English language combined test, you're given a certificate by the further-education college (see the sections on learning English later in this part).

You now have to fill out *Form AN Application for Naturalisation,* which you can find at the Immigration and Nationality Directorate (IND) Web site www.ind.home office.gov.uk. See Part III for more about this form.

Retaking the test

So what happens if you fail the test? Well, you're given the bad news in the test centre. Don't worry – you're not marched off to the airport and put on the first plane home.

In fact, nothing is further from the truth. You can carry on going to work, attending college, living with your partner, or looking after your family. The only thing that's changed is that you haven't met the criteria – yet – for British citizenship. No sweat, you can resit the exam, provided you're willing to pay the fee of £34 again. The next time – fingers crossed – with a bit of careful reading of *British Citizenship For Dummies,* you'll pass the test with flying colours.

If you do fail to pass the test again, try to assess why you didn't quite come up to scratch. Perhaps your weakness is the cultural questions or the governmental questions in the test. Do some more revision on your weakest topics prior to retaking the test.

There's no limit to the number of times you can take the citizenship test. The only limit is how often you can pay out the £34 sitting fee!

Talking About the English Language Requirement

Passing the citizenship test is enough to meet the other requirement for British citizenship, which is to display competence in the English language. However, the other route is to take the citizenship qualification combined with an English language qualification.

In order to be granted citizenship you also need to have lived in the UK for a specific period of time and not to have been in breach of the UK immigration rules at any time. Check out Part I for more on citizenship requirements.

If you are over 65 or have a mental impairment, then it may be possible for you to bypass the citizenship test or citizenship/language requirements and still qualify as a British citizen. It is at the Home Office's discretion whether to grant citizenship without evidence of your ability to speak English and without having passed the Life in the UK test.

Proving competence in English

If your English skills aren't at a sufficient level to pass the citizenship test, in order to prove that you're competent at English you must attain the qualification *English for Speakers of Other Languages (ESOL) Entry Three*.

Chatting in Gaelic or Welsh

Britain is made up of distinct countries: England, Scotland, and Wales, as well as Northern Ireland. English is, by a long way, the main language spoken in the UK. However, Scotland and Wales both have their own national languages – Scots Gaelic and Welsh. If you can prove competence in either of these two languages, then you can pass the language skills part of the citizenship test. In other words, you don't have to be fluent in English if you can speak Scots Gaelic or Welsh.

However, both Scots Gaelic and Welsh are minor languages, spoken by relatively small numbers of people in the UK. If you want to really integrate in British society, you're best advised getting your English up to scratch.

Put simply, ESOL Entry Three demonstrates that you have the ability to hold a conversation on a straightforward topic, such as the weather (a preoccupation amongst the British), or a trip to the shops. You don't have to be word-perfect in your conversation or use exactly the right grammar. To attain ESOL Entry Three, you simply have to get your point across in an understandable way.

Taking an ESOL course

ESOL is taught at colleges. Have a look at the 'Education and learning' section on the Government's public services Web site at www.direct.gov.uk. You can search for a course on this Web site.

Alternatively, to find out more about ESOL and citizenship classes, contact your local college direct (you can find the details in the *Yellow Pages*), or call the Government's Life in the UK test helpline on 0800 015 4245.

Course fees depend on the college you choose to study at, but some offer to register you on an ESOL level 1 course for as little as £10. You can build up through ESOL levels 1, 2, and 3, or you can go straight for level 3. Assessment is by a paper-based test and you are free to ask to be tested at any time. Some courses last a couple of months, with one session a week, while others last six months or a little longer. The rule of thumb is that the longer the course, the more in-depth the citizenship study.

You can have your English assessed at a Learn Direct centre. Learn Direct is an organisation that aims to boost education and skills amongst adults. Learn Direct operates a network of more than 2,000 online learning centres in the UK. They operate a helpline on 0800 101 901 and a Web site at www.learndirect.co.uk.

Celebrating with a Citizenship Ceremony

The British citizenship ceremony has proved a big hit. After all, everyone loves a celebration and that's exactly what the ceremony is.

The ceremony marks the happy event of moving to citizenship and the granting of full voting and other rights. See Part VI for more on what rights citizenship brings.

Attending the ceremony

Citizenship ceremonies are held in town halls and registry offices throughout the country, organised by local authorities. New citizens are invited and can bring along family, friends, and well-wishers. Usually between 12 and 24 new citizens attend each ceremony. The local authority may limit the number of guests you can invite to your ceremony, so check with the organising authority before inviting all your relatives!

Superintendent registrars preside over the ceremony – the same people who conduct civil weddings. As a new citizen, you take an oath of allegiance (see the next section). To add a little more gravitas to the occasion, sometimes local dignitaries, such as the mayor, may attend the ceremony, and the national anthem may be played.

Citizenship ceremonies are compulsory (as if you needed an excuse to party!). After you receive your letter from the Immigration and Nationality Directorate (IND) telling you that you're being granted British citizenship, you have 90 days to attend a ceremony. (The IND can take around five months to process your application for citizenship.) Your local authority will contact you with a date for your ceremony.

Missing your ceremony can be a costly error. If you don't attend a ceremony within 90 days of being told to, you have to go through the whole citizenship application process again, and pay all the fees again. However, you don't have to resit the citizenship test or the citizenship and English language course.

The cost of your citizenship ceremony is included in your nationality application fee, currently £268 for an individual (see Part III for the full list of fees).

Throwing a private party

Some local authorities give you, as a new citizen, the option of your own private ceremony with just friends and family presided over by the registrar. However, privacy comes at a cost. Expect to pay around £100 for a private citizenship ceremony.

Taking the oath of allegiance

At the centre of the citizenship ceremony is the moment when you take the oath of allegiance. Here's the oath:

> I (*name*) swear by Almighty God that, on becoming a British citizen, I will be faithful and bear true allegiance to Her Majesty Queen Elizabeth the Second, Her Heirs and Successors according to law.

> I will give my loyalty to the United Kingdom and respect its rights and freedoms. I will uphold its democratic values. I will observe its laws faithfully and fulfil my duties and obligations as a British citizen.

As you can see, the oath is designed to remind you of the responsibilities of British citizenship.

A religious reference to 'Almighty God' is included in the oath, but this is a very generic reference and can be taken by people from a Christian and non-Christian background. No alternative form of words for atheists is offered.

You won't need to memorise the oath! Generally, the presiding officer reads out the oath and you and the other new citizens simply repeat it.

After you take the oath, you're handed your citizenship certificates. This certificate is both a keepsake and a handy document, because you can use it to get your first British passport (read Part VI for information about getting your passport).

The oath of allegiance is extremely important. It is the moment when you become a British citizen.

Part V

Troubleshooting Your Application

. . . .

In This Part

▶ Looking at what can go wrong

▶ Examining your rights to appeal decisions

▶ Knowing the waiting times involved

▶ Coping with citizenship rejection

▶ Knowing about deportation

. . . .

*H*opefully your path to citizenship will be straight-forward. But you have to deal with a lot of bureau-cracy, and you may be unfortunate enough to encounter instances where you fall foul of immigration rules or simply find yourself at the mercy of an unsympathetic official. To keep your immigration status and your ulti-mate British citizenship ambitions on track, you need to know how to troubleshoot.

In this part, I explain what can go wrong with your immi-gration and citizenship bid and how to go about appeal-ing decisions.

Being Aware of What Can Go Wrong

Part I of this book gives you a good idea of just how complex UK immigration law is. Unfortunately, just to confuse and frustrate matters further, you have to throw human error into the mix. Now, I don't want to scare you off, but I do want to make you aware of potential mishaps.

Here are some of the problems you may encounter with your immigration and citizenship bid:

- ✔ **People can lose vitals forms.** Protect yourself from the authorities' losing your paperwork by making duplicates of all your vital documents, such as your birth certificate, and keeping them safe.

- ✔ **Immigration interviews can go wrong.** At certain stages of the immigration process (such as when you first apply for a visa to come to the UK, or following your marriage to a British citizen), you may be asked to attend an interview. The interview is with an immigration official or, if in your country of origin, an Entry Clearance Officer (ECO). Immigration interviews are not meant to be a witch hunt but sometimes, due to poorly trained staff, or the simple fact that the official is in a bad mood, you can find they can take a nosedive. In the worst-case scenario, the official can accuse you of lying about your application.

The Government-funded Immigration Advisory Service recommends that you register an immediate complaint if you feel you haven't received a fair hearing at a visa interview. Ask to speak to the Entry Clearance Manager – the ECO's boss – and tell him or her of your concerns.

✔ **Officials can make wrong judgement calls.** Immigration law is very complicated and sometimes officials can interpret the law wrongly. According to the IAS, one of the most common errors is when an official tells you that you have no right of appeal against a decision. The answer is to seek a second opinion as to whether you can appeal. Check out Part II for details of charities and other bodies that can help.

Appeals against immigration decisions are handled by the Asylum and Immigration Tribunal. You can find out more about them by visiting www.ait.gov.uk or calling 0845 6000 877.

Understanding Your Right of Appeal

You can appeal against certain immigration decisions but not others.

Decisions you can appeal against include the following:

✔ Refusal of entry to the UK when you arrive at a UK airport or seaport.

✔ Refusal to allow you to vary or extend your leave to stay in the UK.

✔ Refusal to allow you to visit the UK when you plan to visit a family member during your stay. A family member is defined as first cousin or closer.

✔ A decision to have you deported.

The decisions you have no right of appeal against include:

- ✔ Refusal of a visa when you want to come to the UK but are not visiting a family member.

- ✔ You are a student planning to come to the UK to study on a course lasting less than six months.

- ✔ Refusal of a work permit. However, you and your potential employer are free to submit new supporting evidence for the immigration authorities to reconsider your case.

If you want to extend your leave to remain in the UK, you have to apply to do so before your visa expires.

Appealing an immigration decision

The appeals process can be long and laborious, and complex cases can take many months to sort out. You can represent yourself at the appeal hearing, but in serious cases you may need to get legal representation, especially for cases of immigration dispute such as denial of leave to remain. (Part II has the details of legal help you can call upon.)

The time limit for lodging an appeal varies:

- ✔ In cases where an overseas refusal is made – in other words you're denied entry into the UK from your country of origin – you have 56 calendar days to lodge an appeal.

- ✔ With a refusal in the UK you have just 12 working days (not including weekends and Bank Holidays) to lodge an appeal.

- ✔ If you're in detention (you are in custody awaiting deportation), the time limit on appeals is just five working days (not including weekends and Bank Holidays).

You can download appeal forms at the AIT Web site at `www.ait.gov.uk/forms_and_guidance/forms_and_guidance.htm`. You return the forms to the AIT.

You're notified in writing of the date, time, and place of your appeal hearing, and you're sent directions to the hearing centre where your appeal will be heard. If you live outside the UK, the hearing takes place in your absence.

If you're late lodging an appeal you may lose your right to appeal.

Appeals are heard by a legally qualified immigration judge(s). You can have legal representation and can call witnesses. The Home Office is represented at the hearing and explains why your immigration application has been turned down. The judge examines the evidence, both written and oral, and may ask you questions. The judge ultimately comes to a decision called a *determination,* which is sent to you in writing within ten days.

Appeals against the denial of asylum are fast-tracked. Sometimes appeals don't go to a full appeal hearing. Initially appeals are assessed at a 30-minute case management review (CMR) hearing presided over by a judge who has the power to assess an appeal without going to a full hearing.

Finding the right appeal form

You have three main appeal forms to choose from. The forms can all be downloaded from the Asylum and Immigration Tribunal Web site at `www.ait.gov.uk`. Guidance on filling out each form is available on the Web site.

Here's a brief run-down of each appeal form:

> ✔ **Form AIT1:** Use this form if you want to appeal against a decision made in the UK when you are also in the UK.

> ✔ **Form AIT2:** Fill out this form to appeal against a decision made by a visa officer abroad. You use this form in your country of origin.

> ✔ **Form AIT3:** You need this form if you want to appeal against an immigration decision made inside the UK after you've left the UK.

You can find further details on how to make a complaint in the 'contact us' section at the Web sites www.ukvisas. gov.uk and www.ind.homeoffice.gov.uk.

Playing the Waiting Game

When it comes to dealing with immigration and citizenship, sadly you can't wave a magic wand and get instant results. The following sections give you an idea of the waiting times involved.

Hanging on for an immigration decision

Anyone dealing with the UK immigration service can tell you that it's the time officials spend making decisions, rather than administrative errors, that piles on the frustration.

Waiting times for a decision vary according to the individual case and the type of application you're making.

Generally, visa decisions are made quickly – in a matter of weeks or even days.

In more complex cases, such as extending leave to remain, decisions about visas can take weeks or even months. Asylum seekers can wait many months for a decision on getting leave to remain.

The IND Web site gives some broad guidance on how long you can expect to wait for each immigration scenario. Look at `www.ind.homeoffice/applying`.

The IAS advises that if you appeal an immigration decision, you can expect to wait a couple of months for your case to be heard. Asylum *appeals,* however, are now being fast-tracked. A full appeal hearing should take place within four weeks of the appeal's being lodged.

You will be told in writing when your appeal hearing is being held, so be as patient as you can!

Holding out for a citizenship decision

When you pass the citizenship test (Life in the UK test) you're given a confirmation letter at the test centre. If you choose the combined English language and citizenship course route, your college supplies you with a certificate. You then send off the confirmation letter or certificate with your application for citizenship to the Immigration and Nationality Directorate (IND) – see Part III for the ins and outs of this process.

According to the IND you can expect your citizenship application to be checked and processed in around five months.

If you want to check progress on your application or have any questions relating to it, you can call the IND's call centre on 0845 010 5200.

All being well, you're told in a letter from the IND that your application has been accepted. You're then in the home stretch. The final thing you have to do is attend a citizenship ceremony and become a true blue British citizen – congratulations!

Dealing with a Citizenship Rejection

The IND rejects around one in seven applications for British citizenship. The main reason for rejection is if the applicant hasn't lived in the UK for long enough (five years, or three years with a British partner) or has spent a long period of time (450 days) out of the UK during the previous five years.

If you're one of the unlucky ones who is rejected, the IND should explain the reason for your rejection. If you need further clarification, call their call centre on 0845 010 5200.

If you're rejected for British citizenship the first time around, the good news is that you can reapply at a later date.

You may want to use the Nationality Checking Service before submitting any forms to the IND. Many local councils offer a checking service that looks over your application and supporting documents to ensure that everything's in order. See Part II for more on the checking service.

Thinking the Unthinkable: Deportation

Under certain circumstances (such as if you've committed a crime while in the UK), the courts can decide that, as a foreign national, you should be deported from the UK and returned to your country of origin. However, ultimately the Home Secretary, as head of the immigration service, decides whether or not to carry out the court's orders. Alternatively, the move to have you deported can come from the Immigration Service if, for example, you've overstayed on a visa or otherwise are found to have broken the terms of your stay in the UK.

Deportation is relatively rare when compared to the numbers of people departing voluntarily or the 100,000 plus people each year who obtain British citizenship and make the most of life in their new home.

Grounds for deportation include the following situations:

- ✔ You're convicted of a criminal offence in the UK and the trial judge has recommended deportation.

- ✔ You have overstayed your visa.

- ✔ Your claim for asylum has been rejected and you have not left the UK voluntarily.

You are informed in writing by the Home Office that you are going to be removed from the UK.

A detention order is often issued at the same time as a deportation notice. Put simply, a *detention order* means that you are taken into custody, where you remain under lock and key until the time comes for you to be deported.

It's possible for you to appeal deportation. If you find yourself in this position, you need legal help, fast. Part II explains how to obtain appropriate legal representation.

A British citizen or someone with the *right of abode* (see Part I for more on this right) cannot be deported.

Part VI

Reaping the Rewards of Citizenship

*B*ritish citizenship is a passport to an array of rights and privileges. British citizens enjoy freedoms and perks that are the envy of many other countries.

In addition, by choosing Britain as your home, you have the benefit of lots of rights such as free medical treatment and education.

In this part, your rights as a citizen and resident are examined.

Unlike many other countries, such as the United States, Britain doesn't have a Bill of Rights. No single document sets out an individual's rights and what the Government or judiciary can and can't do. Instead, British citizens enjoy a patchwork of protection through many centuries of parliamentary legislation and legal rulings. In addition, Britain does subscribe to the Convention on Human Rights – see the later section 'Examining the Human Rights Act'.

Taking Part in the Democratic Process

Being a British citizen gives you the right to vote in general, local government, and European parliamentary elections – provided you're over the age of 18, are not imprisoned for a criminal offence, and do not have a severe mental health problem.

In order to be able to vote, your name has to appear on the *electoral register,* the list of people who live in a *constituency* (local area) who are eligible to vote.

It's quite simple to get your name on the electoral register. Every year local councils send out forms to all households in their area asking for details of everyone living in the house who is eligible to vote. You can either wait for one of these forms to land on your doormat, or alternatively, you can give your local council a call and ask them to send you a form through the post. You can find the number of your local council in the *Yellow Pages*.

If you don't fill in and return your electoral register form, you can be prosecuted and fined.

You have the right to vote, but that doesn't mean that you have to exercise it.

A whirlwind tour of Parliament

The British parliament consists of an elected House of Commons and the appointed House of Lords. Members of the House of Lords are appointed by the Queen but on the say-so of the Government. The Government – including the Prime Minister – is drawn from the biggest political party or coalition of parties in the Commons.

As far as lawmaking is concerned, the House of Commons is far more important than the Lords. The House of Lords can't overturn legislation passed by the Commons; all it can do is delay the law coming into force for a few months. The upshot of this power merry-go-round is that real political clout is concentrated in the hands of the Prime Minister and Cabinet.

Britain is the world's oldest parliamentary democracy – over 700 years old in fact. Yet in the distant past, only men who owned land had the right to vote. During the 19th century, the right to vote was extended to more and more people, and finally, in 1918, women were given voting rights.

British History For Dummies gives a fascinating overview of political history if you want to find out more.

Perhaps, as a British citizen, you decide to live in another European Union country. In that case you can vote in that country's elections (provided you have registered), or alternatively, you can choose to continue to vote in British elections.

Examining the Human Rights Act

The Convention on Human Rights is the closest thing Britain has to a Bill of Rights and yet it isn't even British! The Convention was drawn up by the European Union, and its provisions were enacted into British law in 1998, through the Human Rights Act. As the name suggests, the Convention guarantees certain basic human rights.

Don't think that prior to the convention being adopted into British law, UK society ignored such things as the right to life or liberty. In fact, in most cases, all the convention has done is to formalise rights that already existed due to centuries of domestic law-making and legal precedent.

As a British citizen, you have

- The right to life, and not to be condemned to death or execution
- The right not to be tortured or treated in an inhumane or degrading way
- The right to liberty and security
- The right to a fair trial and not to be punished without due legal process
- The right to respect for your private and family life
- The right to marry and have a family
- Freedom from discrimination
- Freedom of religion, conscience, and thought
- Freedom of speech
- The right of peaceful assembly and demonstration
- The right to protect your property
- The right to an education

That's a lot of rights!

The Human Rights Act grants *absolute* and *qualified* rights. As a British citizen, you have an absolute right to life, which means you may not be killed for *any* reason, even if you commit a heinous crime. *Qualified rights* try to strike a balance between your rights and the rights of everyone else. For example, you have the right to freedom of speech, but not if you use that freedom to incite discrimination.

Looking beyond the Human Rights Act

The provisions of the Human Rights Act are only a fraction of your rights as a British citizen. A whole plethora of laws grant you extra rights.

You have

- The right to have your personal data protected
- The right to information
- The right to medical treatment
- The right to an education
- The right to work
- The right to a home

The following sections explain these rights in more detail.

The right to have your personal data protected

The 1998 Data Protection Act states that data held about you by government agencies and businesses has to be accurate, secure, and up to date.

What's more, only relevant people should be given your personal data. Therefore, for example, your bank shouldn't get its hands on your medical records.

Personal data includes information such as your medical records, credit reference files, and employment record.

The right to information

The 2000 Freedom of Information Act is relatively new, but it has the makings of a big expansion to the rights of the British citizen. Put simply, this law gives you the right to ask for previously private information from public bodies such as local councils or the Government. For example, you may want to find out how much your council is spending on installing speed bumps in your road, or what your local health authority is forking out on paper clips. Any British citizen is free to put in a Freedom of Information request and expect to have it answered.

When making a request under the Freedom of Information Act, put it in writing. The public body has to have a good reason to refuse to supply you with the information you request.

For more details on how the Act works, check out the Information Commissioner's Web site at www.information commissioner.gov.uk.

The Freedom of Information Act only applies to public bodies, not to businesses or individuals.

The right to medical treatment

The British National Health Service (NHS) has its critics, but nevertheless it offers free healthcare, delivered at the point of need. You have the right to apply to be registered with an NHS doctor – called a *general practitioner* or GP for short. The GP has the right to refuse to add you to his or her list, but you have thousands of GPs to choose from, so finding a local GP to register with won't be a problem.

GPs are the gatekeepers of the NHS. It's up to them to refer you to a hospital for treatment – unless it's an emergency, in which case you go to the accident and emergency department of your local hospital.

The right to medical treatment doesn't only apply to British citizens. Even if you're simply visiting from abroad, you're entitled to treatment if, say, you have an accident. The UK also has an extensive private health service that you can use as long as you're prepared to pay.

The right to an education

Any child living in Britain is entitled to free state education. But with rights come responsibilities – as a parent you are legally obliged to ensure that your children attend a school between the ages of 5 and 16. You don't have to send your children to a state school; you're free to send your child to a private school or even have him or her tutored at home.

The right to work

All British citizens can work without restrictions. Laws guarantee that workers – whether British or from abroad – receive a minimum wage.

Under the minimum wage law, workers over the age of 18 are guaranteed an hourly wage of least £5.35 from October 2006. Younger workers are guaranteed a slightly lower hourly rate of pay. Business owners found to be paying their workers below minimum wage can be prosecuted and fined. The Government also runs job centres to help jobseekers find work.

Citizens of Commonwealth countries, aged 17 to 30, can work in the UK without work permits under the *Highly Skilled Migrant Policy or Working Holidaymaker Scheme.* See Part I for more on coming to the UK to work.

The right to a home

In theory, local authorities are meant to provide homeless Britons with a roof over their heads. But, in reality, local authorities prioritise their housing efforts on those considered *vulnerable.* Typically, to be considered vulnerable you would be one or more of the following: be pregnant, already have children, have a severe mental health problem, be abused where you currently live, be disabled, or be elderly.

Young, childless, single people in good health are at the back of the queue as far as obtaining public housing is concerned.

Under the 1996 Housing Act, local authorities have a duty to provide vulnerable people with accommodation for a minimum of two years.

If you are an asylum seeker, you are entitled to temporary accommodation while your application to remain in the UK is processed. However, asylum seekers are barred from working, which means that you have to make do on very limited state handouts. See Part II for more.

Building up a state pension and claiming benefits

After you become a British citizen and are working you start to contribute *National Insurance (NI)* payments. NI payments are the route to gaining the state pension and other benefits. Contribute enough NI payments and when you reach age 65 you will be able to claim a state pension. Make sufficient NI payments and if you lose your job or become disabled you can claim Jobseekers Allowance and Incapacity Benefit.

For more on pensions and benefits, check out the Department for Work and Pensions' (DWP) Web site at www.dwp.gov.uk.

Getting Your Hands on a British Passport

As a British citizen you're entitled to a shiny new British passport. Owning a passport is a pretty big deal because a British passport allows you to travel to other countries in the European Union without the need to apply for a visa, as well as to many other nations around the globe.

As well as allowing you to travel abroad, a passport acts as identification. Having a ready means of proving who you are is becoming increasingly important. For example, internal flight operators now ask for photo ID before allowing you to board a plane.

A British passport doesn't automatically grant you entry into *every* other country. Some nations demand you obtain a visa and other documentation, such as medical or vaccination certificates, before allowing you in.

Applying for a passport

The UK passport form is available from your local Post Office. The form is straightforward. You're asked for the following information:

- ✔ Your personal details and those of your parents, such as your date of birth.

- ✔ Details of your certificate of naturalisation or registration as a British citizen, including the certificate number and place of issue.

- ✔ Two photographs of yourself, countersigned by a person of standing in the community such as a police officer, doctor, teacher, solicitor, or minister of religion.

   The person countersigning your photographs must be a British or Irish passport holder themselves.

- ✔ A fee of £51 for a first-time British passport.

For more details on any aspect of getting hold of a passport, call the UK passport agency helpline on 0870 521 0410.

If you're applying for your first British passport, you may want to use the Post Office's *check and send* passport service. For a fee of £7, the Post Office examines your form and photograph for any anomalies that can lead to your application being rejected.

Allow at least three weeks for an application for a passport sent through the post to be processed. If you need a passport sooner than that, you have to make an appointment at a passport service office. If you want a passport processed fast, you have to pay a larger fee than if you simply go through the postal or check-and-send route.

Say cheese! Taking a passport photograph

The UK passport agency has recently adopted a tough new approach to applicants' photographs because of enhanced security and immigration checking purposes. The upshot is that people failing to meet the agency's exacting standards have their applications rejected and have to reapply.

Here are a few golden rules of passport photographs:

- ✔ Your hair must be brushed away from your face and no shadow must fall on your face.

- ✔ No smiling – yes, that's right, I said no smiling!

- ✔ The picture must be 45 millimetres high and 35 millimetres wide.

- ✔ You must take the picture against an off-white, cream, or light-grey plain background.

- ✔ The photograph must be a close-up shot of your head and shoulders. The distance from your chin to the crown of your head should be between 29 and 34 millimetres in the photograph.

You have been told!

You can find photo booths in many Post Offices and shopping centres, and lots of photo processing shops can also take passport photos for you.

Part VII

Ten Helpful
For Dummies Books

• •

In This Part

▶ Delving into British and European history

▶ Buying a property in the UK

▶ Starting your own business

▶ Knowing your legal rights

▶ Holding your own at a cricket match

• •

A For Dummies book isn't complete without a fun and informative Part of Tens – a concise list of topical information at your fingertips.

This part gives you a taster of all the *For Dummies* titles available for you to get your hands on if you want to find out more about pretty much any aspect of living and working in the beautiful British Isles.

All the books in this part are published by Wiley and are available from libraries and bookshops nationwide. You can also order them online at www.wileyeurope.com.

British History For Dummies

Written by an Oxford-educated history teacher, *British History For Dummies* by Sean Lang is a fascinating and funny whistle-stop tour through the centuries of British history from the Stone Age through to the present day.

If you want to know more about the class system in Britain, the significance of the royal family, or the importance of politics in British life, this book is for you.

If British history piques your interest and you want to find out more about the UK's influence in a wider context, see Sean Lang's *European History For Dummies*.

London For Dummies

When you arrive in the UK, your first port of call is likely to be one of the airports in London, and as the embassies, Home Office, and immigration service are all based there, you're sure to spend some time in the Big Smoke (London).

London is a fast-moving city – a modern capital steeped in history. You may well need a helping hand to navigate not only the city itself but also the currency you use and travel options you have (such as the famous black taxis and the underground rail system known as the Tube).

London For Dummies by Donald Olsen is a mine of information about the distinctive culture of London, along with must-see sights and experiences. You may also be interested in Donald Olsen's *England For Dummies*.

Buying a Home on a Budget For Dummies

Settling down in the UK almost certainly means eventually buying your own place. *Buying a Home on a Budget For Dummies* by finance expert Melanie Bien is a no-nonsense guide to getting on the property ladder for less.

You'll be amazed at how many options are open to first-time buyers, from pitching in with friends or family, to getting help from your local housing authority. Melanie Bien covers both the legal and practical aspects of becoming a homeowner in the UK, without the use of jargon or estate-agent speak!

When you come to selling a property in the UK, check out Melanie Bien's *Buying and Selling a Home For Dummies*.

Starting a Business For Dummies

After becoming a British citizen, you want to contribute to the country that has welcomed you to its green and pleasant land. If you're a bit of an entrepreneur, why not join the 400,000 others starting up their own business?

Colin Barrow, a seasoned entrepreneur himself, explains all you need to know to make a success of your start-up venture, from preparing a business plan to show to potential investors, to becoming a great manager when you reach the heady heights of employing people to work for you.

After you get your business off the ground, a good accompaniment to this book is Liz Barclay's *Small Business Employment Law For Dummies*.

Tough Interview Questions For Dummies

Starting your own business may not be one of the pressing goals in your life. But you still want to get a good job in the UK, right?

Rob Yeung's book is a life-saver for anyone who wants to be thoroughly prepared when it comes to answering questions from a potential employer whom you want to impress.

You may also want to check out *CVs For Dummies* by Steve Shipside and Joyce Lain Kennedy.

UK Law and Your Rights For Dummies

UK Law and Your Rights For Dummies offers invaluable information and advice for all UK citizens. What rights do you have if you want to return a faulty kettle? What can you do if your partner decides to leave you and take your CD collection with them? What can you do if your neighbour shouts offensive remarks to you every time you open the front door?

Liz Barclay explains everyday legal issues without resorting to mind-boggling jargon. The book shows you how to navigate legal bureaucracy and avoid ending up on the wrong side of the law.

Sorting Out Your Finances For Dummies

When you move to Britain, you move to a land renowned for its financial institutions. The Bank of England is the second oldest bank in the entire world – it was founded in 1694!

You will almost certainly decide to take out a mortgage if you buy a property in the UK, and you may have debts to pay off (after paying all the citizenship fees) or decide you want to start putting some savings aside for the future.

Sorting Out Your Finances For Dummies by Melanie Bien covers a huge range of money matters from finding the best insurance to getting yourself set up with a pension.

Genealogy Online For Dummies

If you become a British citizen and have children, you may want your kids to know their heritage and history. While *Genealogy For Dummies* by Jenny Thomas, April Leigh Helm, Matthew L. Helm, and Nick Barratt, is mainly geared for families with ancestors in Britain, you may find it useful as a starting point for using your computer and the Internet to travel back in time through the centuries.

Gardening For Dummies

Okay, okay, so *Gardening For Dummies* doesn't have a scrap of relevance to becoming a British citizen. But a

Brit's favourite topic of conversation, after the weather and the latest episode of *EastEnders,* is the garden.

This book, by Sue Fisher, Michael MacCaskey, and Bill Marken, takes you right through the gardening year and the planting process, from designing a garden, through to planting bulbs, and composting.

Cricket For Dummies

Written by yours truly, a lifelong fan and captain of two cricket teams, this title is a must if you really want to immerse yourself in authentic British culture.

Say the word 'England' and many people instantly think of a pristine village green, with lean men in white clothes, bowling and batting with reserved determination. More English than tea with milk, *Cricket For Dummies* covers the rules of the game, tips on improving your play, and deciphers cricket-speak so you know your googly from your gully!

Appendix A

Revision Material for the Life in the UK Test

● ●

*T*he three chapters in this appendix are taken from the UK Government publication *Life in the United Kingdom: A Journey to Citizenship*. These chapters (2, 3, and 4) are the only part of the Government publication that you're examined on in the Life in the UK test, which you have to pass to gain British citizenship. If you do want to buy the whole book, you can purchase it from the Government's stationery office for £9.99. Check out www.tsoshop.co.uk for more details.

Read this appendix carefully and memorise as much of the content as you can. Appendix B consists of sample questions (and answers!) in the same vein as the questions you'll be asked in the test.

For more information about the test itself, see Part IV.

Chapter 2: A Changing Society

Migration to Britain

If we go back far enough in time, almost everyone living in Britain today may be seen to have their origins elsewhere. We are a nation of immigrants able to trace our roots to countries throughout Europe, Russia, the Middle East, Africa, Asia, and the Caribbean. In the past immigrant groups came to invade and to seize land. More recently, people have come to Britain to find safety and in search of jobs and a better life.

Britain is proud of its tradition of providing a safe haven for people fleeing persecution and conflict. In the sixteenth and seventeenth centuries, Protestant Huguenots from France came to Britain to escape religious persecution. The terrible famine in Ireland in the mid 1840s led to a surge of migration to the British mainland, where Irish labourers provided much of the workforce for the construction of canals and railways.

Between 1880 and 1910, large numbers of Jewish people came to Britain from what are now Poland, Ukraine, and Belarus to escape the violence they faced at home. Unhappily, in the 1930s, fewer were able to leave Germany and central Europe in time to escape the Nazi Holocaust, which claimed the lives of 6 million people.

Migration since 1945

At the end of the Second World War, there was the huge task of rebuilding Britain after six years of war. With not enough people available for work, the British government encouraged workers from other parts of Europe to help with the process of reconstruction. In 1948, the invitation was extended to people in Ireland and the West Indies.

A shortage of labour in Britain continued throughout the 1950s and some UK industries launched advertising campaigns to attract workers from overseas. Centres were set up in the West Indies to recruit bus crews, and textile and engineering firms in the north of England and the Midlands sent agents to find workers in India and Pakistan. For about 25 years people from the West Indies, India, Pakistan, and later Bangladesh, travelled to work and settle in Britain.

In the 1970s, migration from these areas fell after the Government passed new laws restricting immigration to Britain. However, during this period, Britain admitted 28,000 people of Indian origin who had been forced to leave Uganda, and 22,000 refugees from South East Asia. In the 1980s, the largest immigrant groups were from the United States, Australia, South Africa, New Zealand, Hong Kong, Singapore, and Malaysia.

With the fall of the Iron Curtain and the break-up of the Soviet Union in the late 1980s and early 90s, other groups began to come to Britain, seeking a new and safer way of life. Since 1994 there has been a rise in the numbers moving to Britain from Europe, the Middle East, Asia, Africa and the Indian sub-continent, many of whom have sought political asylum. Migrants to Britain, however, face increasingly tighter controls, as the Government attempts to prevent unauthorised immigration and to examine more closely the claims of those seeking asylum.

The Changing Role of Women

In 19th-century Britain, families were usually large and, in most households, men, women, and children all contributed towards the family wage. Although they were economically very important, women in Britain had fewer rights in law than men. Until 1857, a married woman had no right to divorce her husband, and until 1882 a woman's earnings, along with any property or money she brought to the marriage, automatically belonged to her husband.

In the late 19th and early 20th centuries, an increasing number of women campaigned and demonstrated for greater rights and, in particular, the right to vote. However, the protests and demonstrations were halted during the First World War, as women joined in the war effort and took on a much greater variety of work than they had done before. Women (over the age of 30) were finally given the right to vote and to stand for election for Parliament after the war had ended in 1918. It wasn't until 1928 that women in Britain received voting rights at the same age as men.

Despite these improvements, women still faced discrimination in the workplace. When a woman married, it was quite common for her to be asked to leave work by her employer. Many jobs were closed to women, and women found it very difficult to enter university. The 1960s and 1970s saw increasing pressure from women for equal rights and, during this period, laws were passed giving women the right to equal pay and prohibiting employers from discriminating against women because of their sex.

Women in Britain today

Women in Britain make up 51 per cent of the population, and 45 per cent of the workforce. Girls, as a whole, leave school today with better qualifications than boys, and there are now more women than men at university. Employment opportunities for women now are much greater than they were in the past. Although women continue to be employed in traditionally female areas, such as health care, teaching, secretarial, and sales, there is strong evidence that attitudes are changing and that women are doing a much wider range of work than before.

Research shows that today very few people believe that women in Britain should stay at home and not go out to work. Today, almost three-quarters of women with children of school age are in paid work.

In many households, women continue to have a major share in childcare and housework, but here too there is evidence of greater equality, with fathers taking an increasing role in raising the family and household chores. Despite this progress, many argue that more needs to be done to achieve greater equality between women and men, particularly in the workplace. Women in Britain do not have the same access as men to promotion and better-paid jobs, and the average hourly rate of pay for women is about 20 per cent lower than it is for men.

Children, Family, and Young People

In Britain there are almost 15 million children and young people up to the age of 19. This represents almost a quarter of the UK population. Young people are considered to be a group with their own identity, interests, and fashions that in some ways distinguish them from older people. Generally speaking, once they reach adulthood, children tend to move away from the family home, but this varies from one family and one community to another. Most children in Britain receive weekly pocket money from their parents, and many get more for doing jobs around the house.

Children today in the UK do not play outside the home as much as they did in the past. Home entertainment, such as television, videos, and computers, are seen as part of the reason for this, but so also is an increased concern for children's safety. Incidents of child molestation by strangers are often reported in great detail, but there is no evidence that dangers of this kind are increasing.

As a result of changing attitudes towards divorce and separation, family patterns in Britain have also changed considerably in the last 20 years. Today, while 65 per cent of children live with both birth parents, almost 25 per cent live in lone parent families, and 10 per cent live within a stepfamily.

Education

The Government places great importance on the need to assess and test pupils in order to know what they have achieved. Compulsory testing takes place at the ages of seven, eleven and fourteen in England and Scotland (but not in Wales where more informal methods of assessment are favoured). These tests help to give parents a good indication of their children's progress and children know the subjects they are doing well and those that need extra attention.

Most young people take GCSE (General Certificate of Secondary Education) examinations at 16, and many take vocational qualifications, A/S and A levels (Advanced levels), at 17 and 18.

One in three young people now move onto higher education after school. The Government aim is to reach one in two. Of those that do, some defer their university entrance by taking a year out. This often includes periods doing voluntary work, travelling overseas, or earning money to pay for fees and living expenses at university.

Work

It is now common for young people to have a part-time job whilst they are still at school. Recent estimates suggest that there are two million children at work at any one time. The most common jobs are newspaper delivery and work in supermarkets and newsagents. Many parents believe that part-time work of this kind helps children to become more independent, as well as providing them (and sometimes their family) with extra income.

It is important to note, however, that the employment of children is strictly controlled by law, and that there are concerns for the safety of children who work illegally or are not properly supervised.

Health hazards

Many parents in Britain worry that their children may misuse addictive substances and drugs in some way.

Cigarette consumption in Britain has fallen significantly and now only a minority of the population smoke. Restrictions are planned against smoking in public places. Smoking has declined amongst young people as well as adults, although statistics show that girls smoke more than boys. Tobacco, by law, should not be sold to anyone under the age of 16.

Alcohol abuse is a problem. Although young people below the age of 18 are not allowed by law to buy alcohol, there is concern in Britain over the age at which some young people start drinking, and the amount of alcohol that they consume in one session or 'binge'. Increasing penalties including on-the-spot fines are being introduced to help control this.

Controlled drugs are illegal drugs. It is an offence in Britain to possess, produce, or supply substances such as heroin, cocaine, ecstasy, amphetamines, and cannabis. However, current statistics indicate that half of young adults, and about a third of the population as a whole, have used illegal drugs at one time or another, if sometimes only as an experiment.

There is a well-established link between the use of hard drugs (e.g., crack cocaine and heroin) and crime, and it is widely accepted that drug misuse carries a huge social and financial cost to the country. Much crime, such as burglary or stealing in the street by threat or violence (called mugging) is associated with wanting money for drugs. The task of finding an effective way of dealing with this problem is an important issue facing British society.

Young people's attitudes and action

Young people in Britain are able to vote in elections from the age of 18. However, in the 2001 general election, only one in five potential first-time voters actually cast their vote, and there has been a great debate over the reasons for this. Researchers have concluded that one reason is young people's distrust of politicians and the political process.

Although many young people show little interest in party politics, there is strong evidence that they are interested in some specific political issues. Those who commonly say they are not interested in politics at all often express strong concern about environmental issues and cruelty to animals.

A survey of the attitudes of young people in England and Wales in 2003 revealed that crime, drugs, war/terrorism, racism, and health were the five most important issues that they felt Britain faced today. The same survey asked young people about their participation in political and community events. It was reported that 86 per cent of young people had taken part in some form of community activity over the past year. 50 per cent had taken part in fund-raising or collecting money for charity.

Chapter 3: Britain Today: A Profile

Population

In 2001, the population of the United Kingdom was recorded at just under 59 million people.

UK population 2001:

- England 49.1 million 83% UK population
- Scotland 5.1 million 9% UK population
- Wales 2.9 million 5% UK population
- N Ireland 1.7 million 3% UK population
- Total UK 58.8 million

Source: National Statistics

More information on the 2001 Census is available from the Government Statistics Web site, www.statistics.gov.uk.

Since 1951, the population has grown by 17 per cent. This is lower than the average growth for countries in the European Union (which is 23 per cent), and much smaller than some other countries, such as the USA (80 per cent), and Australia (133 per cent).

The UK birth rate was at an all time low in 2002 and, although it rose slightly in 2003, Britain now has an ageing population. For the first time, people aged 60 and over form a larger part of the population than children under 16. There is also a record number of people aged 85 and over.

Although there has been a general increase in population in the UK over the last 20 years, the growth has not been uniform, and some areas, such as the north east and north west of England have experienced a decline.

The Census

A census of the population in Britain has been taken every ten years since 1801 (with the exception of 1941, when Britain was at war). The next census will be in 2011.

When a census takes place, a census form is delivered to households throughout the country, and by law must be completed. The form asks for a lot of information to ensure that official statistics about the population are accurate, but is all completely confidential and anonymous as regards each individual. Only after 100 years can the records be consulted freely.

Ethnic diversity

The largest ethnic minority in Britain are people of Indian descent. These are followed by those of Pakistani descent, of mixed ethnic descent, Black Caribbean descent, Black African descent, and Bangladeshi descent. Together these groups make up 7.9 per cent of the UK population.

Today, about half the members of the African Caribbean, Pakistani, Indian, and Bangladeshi communities were born in Britain. Considerable numbers of people of Chinese, Italian, Greek and Turkish Cypriot, Polish, Australian, Canadian, New Zealand and American descent are also resident within the UK.

UK population 2001:

- ✔ White 54.2 million 92.0% UK population
- ✔ Mixed 0.7 million 1.2% UK population

Asian or Asian British:

- ✔ Indian 1.1 million 1.8% UK population
- ✔ Pakistani 0.7 million 1.3% UK population
- ✔ Bangladeshi 0.3 million 0.5% UK population
- ✔ Other Asian 0.2 million 0.4% UK population

Black or Black British

- ✔ Black Caribbean 0.6 million 1.0% UK population
- ✔ Black African 0.5 million 0.8% UK population
- ✔ Black Other 0.1 million 0.2% UK population
- ✔ Chinese 0.2 million 0.4% UK population
- ✔ Other 0.2 million 0.4% UK population

Source: National Statistics from the 2001 census

Where do people live?

Most members of ethnic minority groups live in England, where they make up nine per cent of the total population. This compares with two per cent each in Wales and Scotland, and less than one per cent in Northern Ireland.

Forty-five per cent of the population of ethnic minorities live in the London area, where they comprise 29 per cent of all residents. Most other members of ethnic minorities in Britain live in one of four other areas: the West Midlands, the South East, the North West, and Yorkshire and Humberside.

Religion and Tolerance

Everyone in Britain has the right to religious freedom. Although Britain is historically a Christian society, people are usually very tolerant towards the faiths of others and those who have no religious beliefs.

In the 2001 Census, just over 75 per cent of the UK population reported that they had a religion. More than seven people out of ten stated that this was Christian. Nearly three per cent of the population described their religion as Muslim, and one per cent as Hindu. After these, the next largest religious groups are Sikhs, Jews, and Buddhists.

Although many people in Britain have a religious belief, this is not always matched by regular attendance at services. It is estimated that regular church attendance in England is between eight and eleven per cent of the population. Church attendance in Scotland however, although declining, is almost twice the level for England and Wales.

The established church

The Church of England, or Anglican Church as it is also known, came into existence in 1534. The King installed himself as head of the Church, and the title of Supreme Governor has been held by the King or Queen ever since.

The monarch at the coronation is required to swear to maintain the Protestant Religion in the United Kingdom, and heirs to the throne are not allowed to marry anyone who is not Protestant. The Queen or King also has the right to appoint a number of senior church officers, including the Archbishop of Canterbury, who is the head of the Church. In practice however, the Prime Minister makes this selection on the recommendation of a special committee appointed by the Church.

Other Christian groups

Further splits in the Church took place after the Reformation, giving rise to a number of different Protestant denominations. These included the Baptists, Presbyterians, and the Society of Friends (or Quakers), all of which continue today. In the 18th century the Methodist movement developed, working in particular amongst poorer members of society.

In Wales today, Baptists and Methodists are the two most widespread denominations. In Scotland there are more than a million members of the Presbyterian Church, the established Church of Scotland, known as the Kirk.

About ten per cent of the population of Britain are Roman Catholic.

The Regions of Britain

Britain is a relatively small country. The distance from the north coast of Scotland to the south coast of England is approximately 600 miles (almost 1,000 km), and it is about 320 miles (just over 500 km) across the widest part of England and Wales. However, nowhere in Britain is more than 75 miles (120 km) from the coast.

Many people remark on the great variety in the British landscape. In the space of a few hours it is possible to travel from a major cosmopolitan city to historic sites, old cathedrals, villages, moors and mountains.

Regional differences

In one respect, almost every part of Britain is the same. A common language, national newspapers, radio, and television, and shops with branches throughout the United Kingdom mean that everybody, to some degree, shares a similar culture. However beneath the increasingly standardised appearance of our city centres and suburbs, there are real diversities and cultural differences between different parts of the United Kingdom.

Possibly the two most distinctive areas of Britain are Wales and Scotland. Both have their own language. Welsh is taught in schools and widely spoken in north and west Wales. Gaelic is still spoken in the Highlands and Islands of Scotland. Many people believe that the Welsh and the Scots have a stronger sense of identity and culture than the English perhaps brought about by their struggle to stay independent. The creation of the Assembly for Wales and the Scottish Parliament in 1999 has led some people to suggest that England needs its own parliament and there is now considerable discussion about what is a distinctive English identity.

Accents are a clear indication of regional differences in Britain. Geordie, Scouse, and Cockney are well-known dialects from Tyneside, Liverpool, and London respectively, but other differences in speech exist in all parts of the country. Scottish and Welsh speech is distinctive, and varies within those two countries. In some areas a person's accent will indicate where they are from, within a distance of twenty miles.

Regional differences also exist in the styles of buildings and the materials used in their construction. Thatched cottages, much less common than they once were, are mainly products of the south, the south-west and east of England. Older buildings are usually made from local stone, giving houses in North Yorkshire, Derbyshire, and many other places a unique appearance.

The industrial legacy of regions also gives rise to distinct styles of architecture. The mill towns of northern England are good examples of this. The insularity of some communities, particularly on the coast and in remote corners of Britain, has meant that their appearance has changed very little in the past 50 years. In contrast, other areas, whose traditional industries have been replaced by others, are almost unrecognisable from what they were a generation ago.

Customs and Traditions

Tourist guides commonly paint a view of a rural Britain that is not always recognisable to those who live here. The countryside is regarded by many as 'real England', but in fact, the great majority of people live in cities or their suburbs. People's lives in the UK, like many others throughout the world, are a mixture of the old and the new. City dwellers love to visit the countryside. But the abolition of fox hunting, regarded by many city dwellers as long overdue, has been bitterly contested by most country dwellers who see it as a denial of their values and traditions.

Festivals and other traditions continue to exist in all parts of the country, but their existence depends almost entirely on the continued support of those who live in the local community.

Sport

Sport of all kind plays a major part in many people's lives. Football, rugby, and cricket all have a large following, and success on the sporting field is a great source of local and national pride. Major sporting events, such as the Grand National horse race, the Football Association (FA) Cup Final, and the Wimbledon tennis championships, capture the attention of many people in Britain, including those who do not normally follow these sports.

National days

National days are not celebrated in Britain in the same way as they are in a number of other countries. Only in Northern Ireland (and the Republic of Ireland) is St Patrick's Day taken as an official holiday. The greatest celebrations are normally reserved for the New Year and the Christian festivals of Christmas and Easter.

National days:

- 1st March St David's Day, the national day of Wales
- 17 March St Patrick's Day, the national day of both Northern Ireland and the Republic of Ireland
- 23rd April St George's Day, the national day of England
- 30 November St Andrew's Day, the national day of Scotland

There are also four public holidays a year, called Bank Holidays, when legislation requires banks and most businesses to close. These are of no nationalistic or religious significance.

Religious and traditional festivals

Most religious festivals in Britain are based on the Christian tradition, but also widely recognised are customs and traditions such as Eid ul-Fitr, Divali and Yom Kippur, belonging to other religions. Many of these are explained to children in all the schools as part of their lessons in religious education; and they are celebrated by followers of these faiths in their communities.

The main Christian and traditional festivals:

Christmas Day, December 25th, celebrates the birth of Jesus Christ. It is normally seen as a time to be spent at home with one's family. Preparations often begin three or four weeks beforehand, as people decide what presents to buy for close family and friends.

A Christmas tree is usually decorated and installed in the entrance hall or living room, around which presents are placed before they are opened on Christmas Day. Christmas cards are normally sent to family and friends from the beginning of December. Non-Christians usually send cards too, which will often simply say 'Seasons Greetings'. Houses are decorated with special Christmas garlands, and sometimes a wreath of holly on the front door. Mistletoe is often hung above doorways, beneath which couples should traditionally kiss. Christmas is both a religious and a secular holiday, celebrated by believers and non-believers alike. Many families attend a church service, either at midnight on Christmas Eve, or on Christmas morning.

Children hang up a long sock, stocking, or pillowcase at the foot of their bed, or around the fireplace for Father Christmas to fill with presents. On Christmas Day, families traditionally sit down to a dinner of roast turkey, followed by Christmas pudding – a rich steamed pudding made from suet, dried fruit and spices.

The British Father Christmas is a cheerful old man with a beard, dressed in a red suit trimmed with fur. He travels from an area close to the North Pole on a sledge pulled by reindeer, delivering presents to children. The Father Christmas we have today is often said to be based on folklore that Dutch, German, and Swedish settlers brought to America, although there are a number of other rival theories explaining his origins.

Boxing Day, the 26th December, refers to a time when servants, gardeners, and other trades people used to receive money (a Christmas box) in appreciation for the work they had done throughout the year. Many people still give to postmen.

Boxing Day is a holiday in Britain, where people visit family and friends and continue with Christmas festivities. It is also a popular day for sporting activities – weather permitting.

New Year, January 1st, is celebrated in Britain, as it is in many countries throughout the world. Parties or celebrations begin on New Year's Eve, and when midnight arrives everybody cheers and drinks a toast for good luck in the coming year.

In Scotland, New Year can be a bigger festival than Christmas. Here there is a tradition in many homes of first footing, in which the first visitor of the New Year brings in particular items such as coal, bread and whisky intended to ensure prosperity for the coming year.

In Wales, on the stroke of midnight, the back door is opened to release the Old Year. It is then locked to keep the luck in, and at the last stroke, the front door opened to let in the New Year.

Easter, which takes place in March or April, commemorates the Crucifixion and Resurrection of Jesus Christ, although it is named after the Saxon goddess of spring,

Eostre, whose feast took place at the spring equinox. Easter, like Christmas, has become increasingly secular, and often taken as an opportunity for a holiday.

Easter eggs, made from chocolate (traditionally, decorated chicken's eggs) are given as presents, particularly to children, symbolising new life and the coming of spring. Some places hold festivals and fairs on Easter Monday.

Other traditions

St Valentine's Day, February 14th, is the day when boyfriends, girlfriends, husbands, and wives traditionally exchange cards and presents; cards are unsigned as if from secret admirers.

Mothering Sunday, three weeks before Easter, is a day on which children, young and old, remember their mothers by giving them flowers or chocolates and trying to make their day as easy and enjoyable as possible.

April Fool's Day, April 1st, is the day when people may play jokes on one another but only until 12 noon. Sometimes even radio, television, and newspapers try to fool people with fake stories and jokes. The tradition is believed to have originated in sixteenth century France.

Guy Fawkes Night, November 5th, commemorates the Gunpowder Plot in 1605 when a small group of Catholics are said to have plotted to kill the King by blowing up the Houses of Parliament. Soldiers arrested Guido (Guy) Fawkes who was allegedly guarding the explosives beneath Parliament. Today he is remembered with fireworks and the burning of a 'Guy' on a bonfire.

Remembrance Day, November 11th, keeps alive the memory of those who died in both World Wars and in later conflicts. Many people now hold a two minute silence at 11.00am in remembrance of this, for it was at the eleventh hour, of the eleventh day, of the eleventh month in 1918 that the First World War (often called the Great War) finally came to an end.

The terrible fighting in the fields of Northern France and Flanders devastated the countryside and, in the disturbed earth of the bomb craters, it was the poppy that was one of the first plants to re-grow. So this blood-red flower has come to symbolise the sacrifice of those who fall in war.

Today, in the period before Remembrance Day, artificial poppies are sold in shops and on the streets, and many people wear them in their buttonholes in memory of the dead.

Chapter 4: How Britain Is Governed

The Working System

Parliamentary democracy

The British system of government is a parliamentary democracy. General elections are held at least every five years, and voters in each constituency elect their MP (Member of Parliament) to sit in the House of Commons. Most MPs belong to a political party, and the party with the largest number of MPs in the House of Commons forms the government, with the more senior MPs becoming ministers in charge of departments of state or heads of committees of MPs.

The Prime Minister

The Prime Minister (PM) is the leader of the party in power. He or she appoints (and dismisses) ministers of state, and has the ultimate choice and control over many important public appointments. The Prime Minister's leading ministers form the Cabinet. The Prime Minister used to be called (in the lawyers' Latin of the old days) *primus inter pares*, first among equals; but nowadays the office has become so powerful that some people liken it to the French or American Presidency, an office directly elected by the people for a fixed term.

However, a Prime Minister who is defeated in an important vote in the House of Commons, or who loses the confidence of the Cabinet, can be removed by their party at any time. This rarely happens, but when it does, the event is dramatic and the effects can be great. For example, Winston Churchill replaced Prime Minister Neville Chamberlain in 1940; and Margaret Thatcher was forced to resign in 1990, when she lost the confidence of her colleagues.

Modern Prime Ministers have their official residence at 10 Downing Street, and have a considerable staff of civil servants and personal advisers. The PM has special advisers for publicity and relations with the press and broadcasting media all of which adds to the power of the Prime Minister over his or her colleagues. Government statements are usually reported as coming from 'Number Ten'. If something is directly attributed to the Prime Minister it is of special importance.

The Cabinet

The Cabinet is a small committee of about twenty senior politicians who normally meet weekly to decide the general policies for the Government. Amongst those included in the Cabinet are ministers responsible for the economy (the Chancellor of the Exchequer), law and order and immigration (the Home Secretary), foreign affairs (the Foreign Secretary), education, health, and defence. Cabinet decisions on major matters of policy and law are submitted to Parliament for approval.

The British Constitution

To say that a state has a constitution can mean two different things in different countries. Usually it means a set of written rules governing how laws can be made, and setting out the rights and duties of citizens that can be enforced by a constitutional or Supreme Court. But sometimes there is no written constitution so that the term simply describes how a state is governed, what are the main institutions of government and the usual conventions observed by the Government and the politicians.

The United Kingdom constitution is an unwritten constitution. But although no laws passed by Parliament can be directly challenged by any British court, there are restraints on government. Laws define the maximum length of parliaments, the electoral system, qualifications for citizenship, and the rights of non-citizens. There are the rules and procedures of Parliament itself, and interpretations of laws made by the courts in light of the traditions of the common law.

Sovereignty

A fundamental principle of the British constitution is 'the sovereignty of Parliament'. But nowadays decisions of the European Union have to be observed because of the treaties that Britain has entered into; and British courts must observe the judgements of the European Court and the new Human Rights Act. Textbooks are written on 'The British Constitution' and constitutional law, but no one authority will agree fully with another. Some constitutional disputes are highly political such as what should be the composition and powers of the House of Lords and what is the best system of national and local elections.

Some reformers want a written constitution, as does the third largest party at Westminster, the Liberal-Democrats. But others, including the leaders of the Labour and Conservative parties, value historical continuity coupled with flexibility and have no wish for big issues to be settled by a constitutional court, as in the United States and many other democratic countries. But what holds the unwritten system together is that party leaders observe conventions of political conduct.

Conventions

Conventions and traditions are very important in British political life. For example, the second largest party in the House of Commons not merely opposes the Government but is called 'Her Majesty's Loyal Opposition'. It has a guaranteed amount of time in Parliament to debate matters of its own choice, and its rights are defended by the Speaker, who chairs proceedings in the House of Commons.

The Leader of the Opposition has offices in Parliament and receives financial support from the Treasury both for his or her office and for the Shadow Cabinet. These are senior members of the main opposition party who 'shadow' government ministers in different departments. The Leader of the Opposition also has a constitutional status (that is why we use capital letters). He or she stands beside the Prime Minister on formal state occasions, as when the Queen opens Parliament or when wreaths are laid at the Cenotaph in Whitehall on Remembrance Day.

Question Time, when Members of Parliament may ask questions of government ministers, is another parliamentary convention. Questions to the Prime Minister by the Leader of the Opposition are usually lively and combative occasions, often widely reported.

A competitive party system

Under the British system of parliamentary democracy, candidates nominated by political parties, and sometimes individual independent candidates, compete for the votes of the electorate in general elections and by-elections. (By-elections are held to fill a vacancy when an MP resigns or dies in office.) The struggle between the parties to influence public opinion, however, is continual, and takes place not only at election time.

The role of the media

Proceedings in Parliament are now broadcast on digital television and recorded in official reports, known as *Hansard*. Although copies of this are available in large libraries and on the Internet, www.parliament.uk, most people receive their information about political issues and events from newspapers, TV, and radio.

In Britain there is a free press – that is, one that is free from direct government control. The owners and editors of most newspapers hold strong political opinions and run campaigns to influence government policy. All newspapers have their own angle in reporting and commenting on political events. Sometimes it is difficult to distinguish fact from opinion. Spokesmen and women of all political parties put their own slant on things too – known today as 'spin'.

In Britain, the law states that political reporting on radio and television must be balanced. In practice, this means giving equal time to rival viewpoints. Broadcasters are free to interview politicians in a tough and lively fashion, as long as their opponents are also interviewed and treated in more or less the same way.

During a general election, the main parties are given free time on radio and television to make short party political broadcasts. In citizenship lessons in schools young people are encouraged to read newspapers critically and to follow news and current affairs programmes on radio and television.

The Formal Institutions

Government and politics in Britain takes place in the context of mainly traditional institutions, laws and conventions, which ensure the acceptance of electoral or Parliamentary defeat, and peaceful and reasonably tolerant behaviour between political rivals.

The institutional arrangements are a constitutional monarchy, the House of Commons, the House of Lords, the electoral system, the party system and pressure groups, the judiciary, the police, the civil service, local government, and the recent devolved administrations of Scotland, Wales and Northern Ireland, together with a large number of semi-independent agencies set up by the government, nicknamed quangos, and now officially called Non-Departmental Public Bodies.

A constitutional monarchy

Britain has a constitutional monarchy. Others exist in Denmark, Netherlands, Norway, Spain, and Sweden. Under a constitutional monarchy, the powers of the King or Queen are limited by either constitutional law or convention.

In Britain, the Queen or King must accept the decisions of the Cabinet and Parliament. The monarch can express her or his views on government matters privately to the Prime Minister, for example at their weekly 'audience', but in all matters of government must follow the Prime Minister's advice. The Queen or King can only, in a famous phrase, 'advise, warn, and encourage'. There would be a constitutional crisis if the monarch ever spoke out publicly either for or against government policy.

The present Queen has reigned since her father's death in 1952. The heir to the throne is her oldest son, the Prince of Wales. He has let his opinions be publicly known on a range of environmental and other matters, but when he becomes King he will be required to act and speak only in a ceremonial manner. Today there are some who argue that modern Britain should become a republic, with an elected President. However, despite public criticisms of some members of the royal family, the monarchy still remains important and popular among most people in Britain today as a symbol of national unity. People distinguish between the persons of the royal family and the institutions they represent.

The Queen is Head of State of the United Kingdom. She is also monarch or head of state, in both a ceremonial and symbolic sense, of most of the countries in the Commonwealth. The Queen has important ceremonial roles in this country, which include the opening and closing of Parliament. Each year at the beginning of a new parliamentary session she reads by tradition 'the Queen's speech' from a throne in the House of Lords, stating the Government's policies for the next session. Today, however, these are entirely the views of the Prime Minister and the cabinet.

The monarch also gives the letters of appointment to holders of high office within the Government, the armed forces, and the Church of England, but always on the Prime Minister's advice.

The House of Commons

The House of Commons is the centre of political debate in Britain and the ultimate source of power. It shares the huge Palace of Westminster with the House of Lords. In medieval times, the House of Lords was the more powerful, and so you will still hear some commentators call the Commons, the Lower House, and the Lords, the Upper House. Today the Commons can always overrule the Lords who can only delay the passage of new laws.

The MPs who sit in the House of Commons are elected from 645 constituencies throughout the UK. They have a number of different responsibilities. They represent everyone in their constituency, they help create and shape new laws, they scrutinise and comment on what the Government is doing, and they provide a forum for debate on important national issues. If you visit the House of Commons you may find few MPs in the main debating chamber. That is because most work is done in committees – scrutinising legislation, investigating administration, or preparing a report on some important issue.

Visiting Parliament

There are public galleries from which the public may listen to debates in both Houses of Parliament and many committees. You can write to your local MP to ask for tickets. There is no charge, but MPs only have a small allocation of tickets, so requests should be made well in advance. Otherwise, on the day, you can join a queue at the public entrance, but a waiting time of one or two hours is common for important debates. Getting into the House of Lords is usually easier. Ask the police officer at the same entrance where to go. Further details are on the UK Parliament Web site, www.parliament.uk.

The Speaker

The Speaker of the House of Commons is an ordinary MP, respected on all sides, and elected by fellow MPs. He or she has the important role of keeping order during political debates in a fair and impartial way; of representing the House of Commons on ceremonial occasions; and of ensuring the smooth running of the business of the House.

The Whips

The Whips are small group of MPs, appointed by their party leaders, to ensure discipline and attendance of MPs at voting time in the House of Commons. The Chief Whip commonly attends Cabinet or Shadow Cabinet meetings and will negotiate with the Speaker over the timetable and the order of business.

The House of Lords

The House of Lords is in the middle of big changes. Until relatively recently, the members were all peers of the realm; that is hereditary aristocrats, or people who had been rewarded for their public service – for example in war, the Empire or government. They had no special duty to attend the House of Lords, and many did not do so.

In 1957 a new law was passed, enabling the Prime Minister to appoint peers just for their own lifetime. These Life Peers, as they were known, were to be working peers, and were encouraged to attend debates in the House of Lords on a regular basis. Today those appointed as life peers have normally had a distinguished career in politics, business, law, or some other profession. Recently hereditary peers had their general right to attend the House of Lords removed, but were allowed to elect a small number of themselves to continue to attend.

Life peers continue to be appointed by the Prime Minister although, by convention, always include people nominated by the leaders of the other parties. Senior Bishops of the Church of England are automatically members of the House of Lords, as are most senior judges. Life peers also include members of other Christian denominations and of other faiths Jewish, Moslem, Hindu, Sikh, or Buddhist, as well non-believers and humanists. Today the main role of the House of Lords is to examine in detail and at greater leisure new laws proposed by the House of Commons, and to suggest amendments or changes. In this way the Lords may delay – but not prevent – the passage of new legislation.

The House of Lords also frequently debates issues that the Commons pass over or can find no time for. House of Lords' committees also, from time to time, report on a particular social problem or scrutinise some aspect of the workings of government.

To prevent a government from staying in power without holding an election, the House of Lords has the absolute right to reject any proposed law that would extend the life of a Parliament beyond the statutory five-year period. However, if this were ever to happen, the House of Commons could first abolish the House of Lords, who could only delay such an act! This is very unlikely but illustrates how constitutional restraints in the United Kingdom depend more on conventions than on strict law.

The electoral system

Members of the House of Commons (MPs) are elected by a 'first-past-the-post' system. The candidate in a constituency who gains more votes than any other is elected, even if he or she does not have a majority of the total votes cast. In the House of Commons, the Government is formed by the party gaining the majority of the seats, even if more votes were cast in total for the Opposition.

Under this system, the number of seats going to the winner is always proportionately greater than their total vote. For this reason, some people argue that the system should be changed to one or other form of proportional representation, as in Ireland and most parts of continental Europe. However, neither of the main UK parties favours this, saying that large majorities in the House of Commons guarantee strong and stable government, and that PR (proportional representation) would lead to coalitions and instability.

However, the Scottish Parliament and the Welsh Assembly were both set up with different systems of PR to ensure that they were not completely dominated by a single party, as can happen under a 'first past the post' system. Similarly, the use of PR for elections to the Northern Ireland Assembly is intended to stop the Unionist (mainly Protestant) majority of voters from taking all the posts of government, and ensure 'power sharing' with the Irish nationalist (overwhelmingly Catholic) parties. In elections for the European Parliament yet another form of PR was adopted to conform more closely to European Union practice.

The party system and pressure groups

The British political system is essentially a party system in the way that decisions are made and elections conducted. There is only a handful of independent MPs or MPs from smaller parties. The main political parties have membership branches in every constituency throughout Britain. Local party organisations select candidates, discuss policy, and canvas the voters in national, local, and European elections. Annual national party conferences are carefully managed and well publicised events, where general party policy is debated, and where local parties can have a significant effect on the Parliamentary leadership.

Public opinion polls have also become very important to the leadership of each party. Party leaders know that they have to persuade and carry large numbers of the electorate, who are not party members, and who in recent years have become less fixed and predictable in their voting habits.

Political party membership in Britain has been declining rapidly in the last few years, perhaps as a consequence of greater consensus between the parties on the main questions of economic management, both seeking the middle ground so that differences of policy and principle are more difficult to perceive; or perhaps because people now, working longer hours and harder, and enjoying for the most part a greater standard of living, can or will give less time to public service. No one knows if this is a temporary or a long-term change. This, combined with falling turnout in elections, especially among 18–25 year-olds, has become a matter of general concern and is widely discussed in the press and in the broadcasting media.

Pressure groups

Pressure groups are organisations that try to influence government policy, either directly or indirectly. There are many such groups in Britain today, and they are an increasingly important part of political life. Generally speaking, ordinary citizens today are more likely to support pressure groups than join a political party.

Sometimes people distinguish between 'pressure groups' and 'lobbies'. Lobbies or 'interest groups' are seen not as voluntary bodies of ordinary citizens but as the voice of commercial, financial, industrial, trade, or professional organisations.

The judiciary

Since medieval times, judges have prided themselves on being independent of the Crown. Under the British system, judges can never challenge the legality of laws passed by Parliament, but they do interpret legislation and if a law contravenes our human rights, judges can declare it incompatible. The law must then be changed.

As a rule, judges in court normally apply the law in the same way as they have done in the past. This ensures that similar cases are dealt with in a consistent way. However there are times when the circumstances of a case have not arisen before, or when senior judges decide that existing judgements do not reflect modern society. In these situations, by their decisions, judges can create or change the law.

Judges in Britain are appointed by a Government minister, the Lord Chancellor, from nominations put forward by existing judges. The names proposed are those of senior lawyers who are believed to have the ability and judgement to do the job. In the last few years, however, there have been demands – to which the Government is responding – that this process should become more transparent, and clearer to members of the press and public. It is also felt that judges should be more representative of the public at large. Many argue that the judges are drawn from too narrow a section of society and that women and members of ethnic minorities are not sufficiently represented.

The police

The police are organised on a local basis, usually with one force for each county. The largest force is the Metropolitan Police, with its headquarters at New Scotland Yard, which serves London. The police have 'operational independence' – the Government cannot instruct them to arrest or proceed against any individual. But their administration is controlled by police authorities of elected local councillors and magistrates, and by the role of the Home Secretary. An independent authority investigates serious complaints against the police.

The Civil Service

The Government is serviced by a large number of independent managers and administrators, who have the job of carrying out Government policy. They are known as civil servants.

The key features of the civil service are political neutrality and professionalism. Before the mid-19th century, civil servants were appointed by ministers and had to be supporters of the party in power. Civil service reform began in the early 19th century, when the East India Company governed India. To prevent corruption and favouritism, candidates were required to pass competitive examinations. In the 1860s this system was extended to the Home Civil Service and continues with many modifications today.

Members of the British civil service today are permanent servants of the state, working for whatever party is in power. This neutrality is very important, but is sometimes a difficult balance to strike. Civil servants must warn ministers if they think a policy is impractical or even against the public interest, but must ultimately find a way of putting into practice the policies of the elected Government.

Political party officials tend to do everything they can to put Government policy in a favourable light. Civil servants may find themselves in a dilemma if they think that a minister is being too optimistic about the outcome of a particular policy, or asking them to do things specifically to discredit the Opposition. In the past, commentators suspected that civil servants too easily imposed their departmental policies on new ministers; but now the suspicion is often that civil servants can on occasion be pushed into open support for party policies they think to be either impractical or incompatible with other policies.

A major restraint on civil servants from becoming too politically involved is the knowledge that, if a general election brings another party to power, they will have to work with a new Government and an entirely different set of aims and policies. When a General Election is pending or taking place, top civil servants study closely the Opposition's policies so that they are ready to serve a new government loyally.

Local government

Towns, cities, and rural areas in Britain are administered by a system of local government or councils, usually referred to as local authorities. Many areas have both district and county councils, although large towns and cities tend to be administered by a single authority, called a borough, metropolitan district, or city council.

Local authorities are responsible for providing a range of community services in their area – such as education, planning, environmental health, passenger transport, the fire service, social services, refuse collection, libraries, and housing. Today local authorities in England and Wales have considerably less control over the organisation of these services than they did in the past.

What local government is required to do is called 'mandatory services', as decided by central government. Citizens can take them to court if they do not perform them: But there are also 'permissive services', though less than in the past: what they may do if they want to and can afford to do. In England and Wales local authorities may only offer permissive services if empowered to do so by government legislation. However in Scotland, under devolution, local authorities can do anything they are not explicitly forbidden to do. This is a simpler system to understand and operate, but financial constraints make the two systems more similar than might be supposed.

Most of the money for local authority services comes from the Government, provided through taxation. Only about 20 per cent is funded locally through the collection of council tax. There are strict systems of accountability, which determine how local authorities spend their money, and the Government is now beginning to explore how much some local services can be delivered by voluntary community groups. Some see this as diminishing the powers of local government but others see it as a way of involving more ordinary citizens in how their area is run.

Elections for local government councillors are held in May each year. Many – but not all – candidates stand as members of a political party. A few cities in Britain, including London, also have their own elected mayors, with increased powers to manage local affairs. Serving on the local council is still frequently the first step (but less so than in the past) to getting the local party to nominate someone as a candidate for election to the national Parliament or Assembly or to the European Parliament in Strasbourg.

Devolved Administration

In 1997, the Government began a programme of devolving power from central government, with the intention of giving people in Wales and Scotland greater control over matters that directly affect them. Since 1999 there has been an Assembly in Wales, and a Parliament in Scotland, and the Government is now proposing the idea of regional governments in England when there is a clear local demand.

However, policy and laws governing defence, foreign affairs, taxation, and social security remain under the control of the UK Government in London, although these issues may be debated in the Welsh Assembly and the Scottish Parliament.

The National Assembly for Wales

The National Assembly for Wales is situated in Cardiff. It has 60 Assembly Members (AMs) and elections are held every four years. Members can speak in either English or Welsh and all its publications are in both languages. The Assembly does not have the power to make separate laws for Wales but it may propose laws for the decision of the UK Parliament in Westminster. However, it does have the power to decide on many other important matters, such as education policy, the environment, health services, transport and local government, where the present laws allow Welsh ministers a great deal of discretion in making detailed regulations.

The Parliament of Scotland

The Parliament of Scotland in Edinburgh arose as the result of a long campaign by people in Scotland for more independence and democratic control. For a long time there had been a devolved administration run by the

Scottish Office, but no national elected body. A referendum for a Scottish Parliament, in 1979, did not gain enough support, but when another was held in 1997, the electorate gave a clear 'yes' both to establishing a Scottish Parliament and to it having limited powers to vary national income tax.

Today there are 129 Members of the Scottish Parliament (MSPs) in Edinburgh, who are elected by a form of proportional representation. Unlike the Welsh Assembly, the Scottish Parliament may pass legislation on anything not specifically reserved to Westminister (foreign affairs, defence, general economic policy, and social security).

The Scottish Parliament is funded by a grant from the UK Government and can spend it how it chooses. It has the legal power to make small changes in the lower base rate of income tax, which it has not exercised so far, and has adopted its own procedures for debate, the passage of legislation and access to the public – all deliberately different from the traditional ways of Westminster.

The Northern Ireland Assembly

The Northern Ireland Parliament, often called Stormont after the building where it met, was established in 1922, following the division of Ireland after civil war. Protestant political parties, however, dominated the Parliament, and abolished the electoral system of proportional representation that was designed to protect the Catholic minority – a community who faced considerable discrimination in housing and jobs in the public services.

The Government in London paid little attention to these problems until, 50 years later, protests, riots, and a civil disobedience campaign led them to abolish Stormont when reforms failed to materialise. Conflicts increased between Protestant and Catholic groups, the former determined to remain part of the United Kingdom, while the latter determined to achieve unity with the Irish Republic.

There followed many years of communal distrust, violence, and terrorism. But after a negotiated cease-fire by both the main para-military groups – the IRA (the Irish Republican Army), and the UDA (the Ulster Defence Association) – the Good Friday Agreement was signed in 1998 between the main parties and endorsed by the Irish and British governments, working closely together.

Shortly afterwards, the Northern Ireland Assembly was established, with a power-sharing agreement in which the main parties divided the ministerial offices between them. The Assembly has 108 elected members, with powers to decide on matters such as education, agriculture, environment, health, and social services in Northern Ireland.

In view of the political situation in Northern Ireland, the UK government kept the power to suspend the Assembly if the political leaders could no longer agree to work together or if the Assembly was not working in the interests of the people of Northern Ireland. This has happened on a number of occasions.

Non-departmental public bodies

Much of government that affects us all is conducted not directly, but through a multitude of agencies with various degrees of independence. These are organisations that Parliament can create or abolish, or change their powers and roles, but are not a direct part of the civil service. They are sometimes called quangos – quasi-autonomous non-governmental organisations.

A few examples of non-departmental public bodies:

- ✔ **Trading bodies set up by central government that raise revenue:** Her Majesty's Stationery Office (official and semi-official publications), Forestry Commission, National Savings Bank, Crown Estates Commission.

- ✔ **Spending agencies funded by government:** Regional Health Authorities, Higher Education Funding Councils, Sports Council, Arts Council, Legal Services Commission, Medical Research Council.

- ✔ **Quasi-judicial and prosecuting bodies:** Monopolies and Mergers Commission, Criminal Injuries Compensation Authority, Police Complaints Authority, Crown Prosecution Service.

- ✔ **Statutory Advisory Bodies to Ministers:** Gaming Board, Health and Safety Commission, Law Commission, Commission for Racial Equality, Equal Opportunities Commission, Advisory Board on Naturalisation and Integration.

- ✔ **Development agencies (many of which are public-private partnerships):** Scottish Enterprise, Highlands and Islands Development Board (Scotland), Welsh Development Agency, Rural Development Commission, several regional Urban Development Corporations.

Britain in Europe and the World

In addition to Britain's historical and cultural ties with countries throughout Europe, two major developments have occurred since the end of the Second World War in 1945 closely linking Britain to the remainder of Europe.

The Council of Europe

The Council of Europe was created in 1949, and Britain was one of the founder members. It is an organisation with 50 member states, working to protect human rights and seek solutions to problems facing European society today. The Council of Europe has no power to make laws, but does draw up conventions and charters, which states agree to follow. Examples of these are the European Convention on Human Rights, measures to trace the assets associated with organised crime, and a directive for education for democratic citizenship in schools.

The European Union

The European Union originated in the period immediately after the Second World War when Belgium, France, Luxembourg, the Netherlands, and West Germany signed an agreement putting all their coal and steel production under the control of a single authority. An important reason for doing this was the belief that co-operation between these states would reduce the likelihood of another European war.

Britain refused to join this group at the beginning and only became part of the European Union (or European Economic Community, as it was then known) in 1973 after twice being vetoed by France. In 2004, ten new member countries joined the EU bringing membership to a total of 25.

The main aim behind the European Union today is for member states to become a single market. To achieve this, measures have gradually been introduced to remove tariff barriers and to help people, goods, and services move freely and easily between member states. This has involved a great deal of regulation being imposed on businesses and consumers, and has not always been popular.

Citizens of a EU member state have the right to travel to any EU country as long as they have a valid passport or identity card. This right may be restricted only for reasons of public health, public order, or public security. They also have the right to work in other EU countries, and must be offered employment under the same conditions as citizens of that state.

The Council of Ministers

The Council of Ministers is one of the most influential bodies in the EU. It is made up of government ministers meeting periodically from each member state with powers to propose new laws and take important decisions about how the EU is run.

The European Commission

Based in Brussels, the European Commission is rather like the civil service of the European Union, taking care of the day to day running of the organisation. One of the important jobs of the European Commission is to draft proposals for new EU policies and law.

The European Parliament

The European Parliament meet in Strasbourg in northeastern France. Each country elects members roughly proportional to its population. Elections for Members of the European Parliament (MEPs) are held every five years.

The Parliament scrutinises and debates the proposals, decisions, and expenditures of the Commission, but does not decide policy. MEPs have the ultimate power to refuse to agree EU expenditure, but have never done so – although they have held it up. Yet the threat has proved effective on several occasions.

European Union law

European Union law is an important source of law in Britain. EU legislation consists mainly of Regulations and Directives. Regulations are specific rules, such as those limiting the hours that drivers of goods vehicles can work, which automatically have the force of law in all EU member states. Regulations override national legislation and must be followed by the courts in each member state.

Directives are general requirements that must be introduced within a set time, but the way in which they are implemented is left to each member state. An example of this is the procedures that must be followed by companies when making staff redundant.

All proposals for new EU laws are examined by a committee of the UK Parliament, which then recommends any changes or amendments to ministers, who will decide whether to try and change or renegotiate them.

The Commonwealth

The Commonwealth arose out of the former British Empire that once included much of Africa and the West Indies, Canada, the Indian sub-continent, Australia and New Zealand. Since 1945, almost all these countries have become independent and together form a loose association called the Commonwealth, with the Crown at its symbolic head.

Only the United Nations is a larger international organisation than the British Commonwealth. The Commonwealth has a membership of 54 states, which together contain 1.7 billion people – 30 per cent of the world's population. Its aims include the development of democracy, good government, and the eradication of poverty, but it has no power over its members other than that of persuasion and only rarely acts together on international issues.

A common language, similarities in culture, and (with some exceptions) mutual recognition of professional qualifications, has greatly assisted the movement of people within the Commonwealth, and had a major effect on migration both to and from Britain.

The United Nations

Britain, like most countries in the world, is a member of the United Nations (UN) – an international organisation, working to prevent war and to maintain international peace and security. Britain is a permanent member of the UN Security Council. The functions of this group include recommending action by the UN in the event of international crises and threats to peace.

Two very important documents produced by the United Nations are the Universal Declaration of Human Rights and the UN Convention on the Rights of the Child. Britain has signed and ratified both of these agreements. Although neither have the force of law, they are important measures by which the behaviour of a state can be judged, and they are increasingly used both in political debate and in legal cases, to reinforce points of law.

The Ordinary Citizen

The right to vote

How does the ordinary citizen connect to government? As we have seen, full democracy came slowly to Britain. Only in 1928 did both men and women aged 21 and over gain the right to vote. The present voting age of 18 was set in 1969.

Both British-born and naturalised citizens have full civic rights and duties (such as jury service), including the right to vote in all elections, as long as they are on the electoral register. Permanent residents who are not citizens have all civil and welfare rights except the right to hold a British passport and a general right to vote.

The electoral register

In order to vote in a parliamentary, local, or European election, you must have your name on the register of electors, known as the electoral register. If you are eligible to vote you may register at any time by contacting your local council election registration office. Voter registration forms are also available, in English, Welsh, and a number of other languages, via the Internet from the Electoral Commission, www.electoralcommission.org.uk.

However the electoral register is also updated annually and an electoral registration form is sent to all households in September or October each year. The form should be completed according to the instructions, and should include everyone eligible to vote who is resident in the household on 15th October.

By law, a local authority has to make the electoral register available for anyone to look at. The register is held at the local electoral registration office (or council office in England and Wales) and some public buildings, such as libraries (however this is not always possible as new regulations require that any viewing of the electoral register is supervised, and libraries do not always have the necessary resources).

You have the right to have your name placed on the electoral register if you are aged 18 or over and a citizen of the United Kingdom, the Commonwealth, or a European

Union member state. Citizens of the United Kingdom, the Commonwealth, and the Irish Republic resident in this country may vote in all public elections. Citizens of EU states, resident in the UK, have the right to vote in all but national parliamentary elections.

Participation

The number of people turning out to vote in parliamentary elections in Britain has been falling for several years, especially amongst the young. In the General Election of 2001, less than half of voters below the age of 25 actually voted. The Government and the political parties are looking for ways in which this trend might be reversed.

Standing for office

Citizens of the United Kingdom, the Irish Republic, or the Commonwealth, aged 21 or over, may stand for public office. However, there are some exceptions, which include peers, members of the armed forces, civil servants, and those found guilty of certain criminal offences.

To become a local councillor, a candidate must have a local connection with the area, through work, by being on the electoral register, or through renting or owning land or property.

This rule, however, does not apply to MPs, MEPs, or to members of the Scottish Parliament, or the Welsh or Northern Ireland Assemblies. Candidates standing for these bodies must pay a deposit of £500, which is not returned if they receive less than five per cent of the vote. The deposit for candidates standing as a Member of the European Parliament is £5,000. This is to discourage frivolous or hopeless candidates, though many still try their luck.

Contacting elected members

All elected members have a duty to serve and represent the interests of their constituents. Contact details of all your representatives and their parties are available from the local library. Those of Assembly Members, MPs, and MEPs are listed in the phone book and Yellow Pages. An MP may be reached either at their constituency office or their office in the House of Commons by letter or phone. The address: House of Commons, Westminster, London SW1A 0AA, tel. 020 7219 3000.

Many Assembly Members, MPs, and MEPs hold regular local 'surgeries', often on Saturday mornings. These are generally advertised in the local paper, and allow constituents to call in person to raise matters of concern. You can also find out the name of your local MP and get in touch with them by fax through the Web site, www. writetothem.com. This service is free.

Appendix B

Sample Questions and Answers for the Life in the UK Test

. . . .

*T*his appendix gives you an accurate example of the types of questions that crop up in the Life in the UK test. These aren't the exact questions that will appear in your test, but they do cover similar information.

These questions are based on the information covered in Appendix A.

Part IV covers the ins and outs of taking, and retaking, the test. In the Life in the UK test, you must get around 18 of the 24 questions correct to pass the test and become a British citizen.

You can find the answers to these multiple-choice questions at the end of this appendix – but no cheating, now!

Good luck with your test!

Questions Based on Chapter 2 in Appendix A

1. Why do migrants come to the UK?

　　a) To claim benefits

　　b) To escape persecution in their own country

　　c) To find safety and in search of jobs and a better life

　　d) To embark on a course of study

2. Why did the Protestant Huguenots come from France to the UK in the 16th and 17th centuries?

　　a) To join the UK in a war with France

　　b) For the excellence of local cuisine

　　c) To find jobs

　　d) To escape religious persecution

3. Why did Irish migrants arrive in the 1840s?

　　a) In response to the potato famine

　　b) The industrial revolution meant there were many jobs in the UK

　　c) As a staging post on their way to the United States

　　d) Because Ireland was in civil war

4. **Which three countries did Jewish people come to the UK from to escape violence they faced at home between 1890–1910?**

   a) France, Italy, and Germany

   b) Poland, Ukraine, and Belarus

   c) Russia, Sweden, and Finland

   d) Syria, Lebanon, and Jordan

5. **In the 1980s the largest immigrant groups came from which countries?**

   a) Poland, Czech Republic, Hungary, Lithuania, and Estonia

   b) Caribbean, Bangladesh, India, and South Asia

   c) United States, Australia, South Africa, New Zealand, Hong Kong, Singapore, and Malaysia

   d) Spain, Italy, France, Portugal, Greece, Malta, and Cyprus

6. **In the 1950s centres were set up in the West Indies to recruit workers for which occupations and industries?**

   a) Bus crews, textile, and engineering

   b) Agriculture, fishing, and rubbish disposal

   c) Legal profession, media, and education

   d) Healthcare, civil service, and publishing

7. **Since 1994 there has been a rise in the numbers moving to Britain from which parts of the world?**

   a) United States, Western Europe, and Australasia

   b) Latin and Central America

   c) Scandinavia and Nordic countries

   d) Europe, the Middle East, Asia, Africa, and Indian subcontinent

8. **Recently the UK has introduced tighter immigration controls. Why?**

   a) To prevent terrorists from entering the UK

   b) To prevent unauthorised immigration and examine the claims of those seeking asylum more closely

   c) To properly verify that those coming to the UK can support themselves and won't prove a burden on the state

   d) To stop the smuggling of alcohol and tobacco products into the UK

9. **In the late 19th and early 20th centuries many UK women demonstrated for what right?**

   a) The right to vote

   b) The right to an abortion

   c) Equal pay and fairer treatment at work

   d) The right to be able to serve in the military

10. **When did British women first get the right to vote?**

    a) 1908

    b) 1918

    c) 1928

    d) 1938

11. **In what year was the voting age for women equalised with that of men?**

    a) 1908

    b) 1918

    c) 1928

    d) 1938

12. **In what year did married women gain the right to divorce?**

    a) 1857

    b) 1887

    c) 1907

    d) 1937

13. **What percentage of the UK population are women?**

    a) 49 per cent

    b) 50 per cent

    c) 51 per cent

    d) 52 per cent

14. **What percentage of the UK workforce are women?**

   a) 45 per cent

   b) 50 per cent

   c) 55 per cent

   d) 60 per cent

15. **What proportion of women with children of school age are in paid work?**

   a) One-quarter

   b) Half

   c) Three-quarters

   d) All of them

16. **By what percentage is the average hourly pay rate of women lower than men's?**

   a) 5 per cent

   b) 10 per cent

   c) 15 per cent

   d) 20 per cent

17. **How many young people, up to the age of 19, are there in the UK?**

   a) 5 million

   b) 15 million

   c) 25 million

   d) 35 million

18. **What proportion of children live with both birth parents?**

    a) 85 per cent

    b) 75 per cent

    c) 65 per cent

    d) 55 per cent

19. **In English and Scottish schools children are given compulsory tests at which ages?**

    a) 5,7, and 9

    b) 7, 11, and 14

    c) 12, 14, and 16

    d) 14, 16, and 18

20. **At age 16 most young people take GCSEs. What does GCSE stand for?**

    a) General Certificate of Secondary Erudition

    b) Great Certificate of Secondary Education

    c) Great Certificate of Secondary Erudition

    d) General Certificate of Secondary Education

21. **At age 17 and 18 many young people in the UK take what type of qualification?**

    a) A/S and A levels as well as vocational qualifications

    b) Driving test examination

    c) Bronze swimming certificate

    d) International baccalaureate

22. **What proportion of young people move onto higher education?**

   a) About one in ten

   b) About one in five

   c) About a third

   d) About a half

23. **How many children work in the UK?**

   a) None, it's against the law

   b) About a million

   c) About two million

   d) About five million

24. **What are the most common jobs young people do?**

   a) Mining and textile work

   b) Newspaper delivery and work in supermarkets and newsagents

   c) Advertising and media

   d) Healthcare and the legal profession

25. **What is the minimum age for buying alcohol?**

   a) There is no minimum age

   b) 16

   c) 18

   d) 21

26. What is the minimum age for buying tobacco?

   a) There is no minimum age

   b) 16

   c) 18

   d) 21

27. Amongst young people, do girls smoke more than boys, or boys more than girls?

   a) Girls smoke more than boys

   b) Boys smoke more than girls

   c) Smoking is banned in the UK

   d) Girls are not allowed to smoke but boys are

28. What proportion of young adults have used illegal drugs at least once?

   a) Around a quarter

   b) Around half

   c) Around three-quarters

   d) Nearly all

29. What is the minimum voting age in the UK?

   a) There is no minimum voting age

   b) 16

   c) 17

   d) 18

30. **What proportion of potential first-time voters actually cast their vote in the 2001 general election?**

    a) Eight out of ten

    b) Five out of ten

    c) Four out of ten

    d) Two out of ten

31. **Name the main reason given by researchers why so few potential first-time voters actually cast their vote.**

    a) Polling stations aren't open late enough

    b) Distrust of politicians and the political process

    c) Not aware that election was taking place

    d) Everything is fine so why bother voting?

32. **Name the five key political issues that young people in the UK say they are most concerned by.**

    a) Jobs, healthcare, education, taxation, and defence

    b) Foreign policy, environment, pensions, jobs, and education

    c) Crime, drugs, war/terrorism, racism, and health

    d) Defence, crime, healthcare, taxation, and pensions

33. **What percentage of young people have taken part in a community activity over the past year?**

    a) 6 per cent

    b) 36 per cent

    c) 56 per cent

    d) 86 per cent

34. **What proportion of young people have collected for charity or taken part in a fund-raising event in the past year?**

    a) A quarter

    b) A third

    c) Half

    d) Three-quarters

35. **During the 1970s, the British Government admitted into Britain approximately how many people of Indian origin who were forced to leave Uganda because of persecution?**

    a) None

    b) 8,000

    c) 28,000

    d) 208,000

36. **When did the Soviet Union break up and people begin to come to Britain from Eastern Europe to seek a better life?**

    a) Late 1990s to early 2000s

    b) Late 1980s to early 1990s

    c) Late 1970s to early 1980s

    d) Late 1960s to early 1970s

37. **In what year did married women gain the right to hold onto their own earnings and property?**

    a) 1882

    b) 1902

    c) 1922

    d) 1942

38. **In which two decades did British society see increasing pressure from women for equal rights, and laws were passed entitling them to equal pay with men?**

    a) 1990s and 2000s

    b) 1980s and 1990s

    c) 1970s and 1980s

    d) 1960s and 1970s

39. **In which year did the First World War end?**

    a) 1908

    b) 1918

    c) 1928

    d) 1938

40. **What did women do in large numbers during the First World War?**

    a) Stay at home and look after the house

    b) Fight and die on the Western Front

    c) Demonstrate against the war and call for peace talks

    d) Took on a much greater variety of work than they had done before, to help the war effort

41. What proportion of children live with both birth parents?

   a) 5 per cent

   b) 35 per cent

   c) 65 per cent

   d) 75 per cent

Questions Based on Chapter 3 in Appendix A

42. What was the total population of the UK in 2001?

   a) 60.8 million

   b) 58.8 million

   c) 56.8 million

   d) 54.8 million

43. What was the population of England in 2001?

   a) 30.4 million

   b) 41.6 million

   c) 45.5 million

   d) 49.1 million

44. What was the population of Scotland in 2001?

   a) 5.1 million

   b) 6.5 million

   c) 7.2 million

   d) 12 million

45. What was the population of Wales in 2001?

    a) 1.7 million

    b) 2.3 million

    c) 2.9 million

    d) 5.2 million

46. What was the population of Northern Ireland in 2001?

    a) 1.1 million

    b) 1.7 million

    c) 2.6 million

    d) 3.8 million

47. The UK population has grown by what percentage since 1951?

    a) 7 per cent

    b) 17 per cent

    c) 27 per cent

    d) 37 per cent

48. Is it true or false that there are now more people aged 60 and over than children under 16?

    a) True

    b) False

    c) They are equal

    d) There are no figures for different age groups

49. **Name two parts of the UK that have seen their populations fall over the last 20 years.**

    a) London and south east

    b) South-west England and Wales

    c) The Midlands and London

    d) The north west and north east of England

50. **In what year was the first census of the UK population carried out?**

    a) 1801

    b) 1851

    c) 1901

    d) 1951

51. **The next UK census will be when?**

    a) 2008

    b) 2009

    c) 2010

    d) 2011

52. **How often is the census carried out?**

    a) Every year

    b) Every 5 years

    c) Every 10 years

    d) Every 20 years

53. **When do census records become available to be consulted freely?**

    a) Immediately

    b) 10 years after the census is conducted

    c) 100 years after the census is conducted

    d) You are not allowed to consult the census records

54. **What is the largest ethnic minority in the UK?**

    a) People from Eastern Europe

    b) People of Caribbean descent

    c) People of Indian descent

    d) People from the United States

55. **What proportion of the African Caribbean, Pakistani, Indian, and Bangladeshi communities were born in the UK?**

    a) About half

    b) About a third

    c) About a quarter

    d) About one-tenth

56. **Ethnic minorities make up what percentage of the UK population?**

    a) 5.6 per cent

    b) 7.9 per cent

    c) 9.1 per cent

    d) 13.5 per cent

57. Ethnic minorities make up what percentage of the English population?

    a) 5 per cent

    b) 8 per cent

    c) 9 per cent

    d) 12 per cent

58. Ethnic minorities make up what percentage of the Welsh and Scottish population?

    a) 2 per cent

    b) 4 per cent

    c) 6 per cent

    d) 8 per cent

59. Ethnic minorities make up what percentage of the Northern Ireland population?

    a) Less than 1 per cent

    b) 3 per cent

    c) 5 per cent

    d) 7 per cent

60. What percentage of ethnic minorities live in London?

    a) 10 per cent

    b) 23 per cent

    c) 37 per cent

    d) 45 per cent

61. What percentage of London's residents are from ethnic minorities?

    a) 6 per cent

    b) 21 per cent

    c) 29 per cent

    d) 42 per cent

62. In the 2001 census, what percentage stated that their religion was Christian?

    a) Around 90 per cent

    b) Around 70 per cent

    c) Around 60 per cent

    d) Around 50 per cent

63. After Christianity what are the two next most common religions in the UK?

    a) Muslim and Hindu

    b) Jedi and Voodoo

    c) Buddhist and Shinto

    d) Jewish and Sikh

64. Is church attendance more common in Scotland, Wales, or England?

    a) Scotland

    b) Wales

    c) England

    d) All about the same

65. **When did the Church of England come into existence?**

    a) 1066

    b) 1534

    c) 1837

    d) 1918

66. **Who holds the title 'supreme governor' of the Church of England?**

    a) The Prime Minister

    b) The Archbishop of Canterbury

    c) The Pope

    d) The Queen

67. **Who is head of the Church of England?**

    a) The Prime Minister

    b) The Archbishop of Canterbury

    c) The Pope

    d) The Queen

68. **What percentage of the UK population are Catholic?**

    a) About 10 per cent

    b) About 20 per cent

    c) About 30 per cent

    d) About 40 per cent

69. **What is the distance from the north coast of Scotland to the south coast of England?**

   a) Approximately 400 miles

   b) Approximately 600 miles

   c) Approximately 800 miles

   d) Approximately 1,000 miles

70. **How wide is the widest part of the UK?**

   a) 120 miles

   b) 220 miles

   c) 320 miles

   d) 520 miles

71. **In which parts of Wales is the Welsh language widely spoken?**

   a) North and west Wales

   b) South and mid-Wales

   c) Anglesey and the Marches

   d) Mumbles and Cardiff

72. **The Scottish Gaelic language is spoken in which parts of Scotland?**

   a) Glasgow and Edinburgh

   b) Lowlands and Border region

   c) West coast and the Isle of Mull

   d) Highlands and Islands

73. In what year was the Assembly for Wales created?

    a) 1999

    b) 2001

    c) 2003

    d) 2005

74. In which year was the Scottish Parliament created?

    a) 1997

    b) 1999

    c) 2001

    d) 2003

75. Does England have its own parliament?

    a) There is no parliament based in England

    b) Yes, it is the House of Parliament in Westminster

    c) No, but it does host the UK parliament in Westminster

    d) Yes, and it also hosts the UK parliament in Westminster

76. Regional accents are common in the UK. Name the well-known dialect for people from London.

    a) Cockney

    b) Scouse

    c) Geordie

    d) Brummie

77. **Name a well-known dialect for people from Liverpool.**

    a) Scouse

    b) Cockney

    c) Geordie

    d) Brummie

78. **Name a well-known dialect for people from Tyneside.**

    a) Cockney

    b) Scouse

    c) Geordie

    d) Brummie

79. **Thatched cottages are mainly produced in what part of the UK?**

    a) South, south west, and south east of England

    b) North east of England

    c) North west of England

    d) Midlands

80. **Which one of these four isn't a major UK sporting event?**

    a) Grand National

    b) Football Association Cup Final

    c) Breeder's Cup

    d) Wimbledon tennis championship

81. **Name three sports played in Britain that enjoy a large regular spectator following.**

    a) Football, cricket, and rugby

    b) Handball, lacrosse, and rowing

    c) Sumo, gridiron, and baseball

    d) Triathlon, downhill skiing, and bobsleigh

82. **Name the patron saint of Wales.**

    a) St Patrick

    b) St David

    c) St Andrew

    d) St George

83. **On what date is the national day of Wales celebrated?**

    a) 30th November

    b) 23rd April

    c) 17th March

    d) 1st March

84. **Name the patron saint of Northern Ireland and Ireland.**

    a) St Patrick

    b) St David

    c) St Andrew

    d) St George

85. **On what date is the national day of Northern Ireland and Ireland?**

   a) 30th November

   b) 23rd April

   c) 17th March

   d) 1st March

86. **Name the patron saint of England.**

   a) St Patrick

   b) St David

   c) St Andrew

   d) St George

87. **On what date is the national day of England?**

   a) 30th November

   b) 23rd April

   c) 17th March

   d) 1st March

88. **Name the patron saint of Scotland.**

   a) St Patrick

   b) St David

   c) St Andrew

   d) St George

89. **What day is the national day of Scotland?**

   a) 30th November

   b) 23rd April

   c) 17th March

   d) 1st March

90. How many public holidays, called Bank Holidays, are there each year throughout the UK?

   a) None

   b) Two

   c) Four

   d) Ten

91. What date is Christmas Day?

   a) 5th November

   b) 1st April

   c) 26th December

   d) 25th December

92. What does Christmas Day celebrate?

   a) The birth of Jesus Christ

   b) The death and resurrection of Jesus Christ

   c) The end of the year

   d) Sales starting in the shops

93. The meat of what bird is traditionally eaten on Christmas Day?

   a) Turkey

   b) Chicken

   c) Ostrich

   d) Penguin

94. Christmas puddings are made of what?

    a) Chopped meat and onion

    b) Vegetables and garlic

    c) Suet, dried fruit, and spices

    d) Fresh fruit and cream

95. In folklore, the character Father Christmas travels from where to deliver presents at Christmas?

    a) Scotland

    b) Denmark

    c) Iceland

    d) Near the North Pole

96. The origins of the Father Christmas character are said to be what?

    a) Pagan folklore from ancient Britain

    b) Invented by the Romans

    c) Invented by the medieval Christian church to persuade children to behave themselves

    d) Folklore taken to America by Swedish, German, and Dutch migrants

97. What date is Boxing Day?

    a) 24th December

    b) 26th December

    c) 31st December

    d) 1st January

98. What traditionally do Britons do on Boxing Day?

a) Stay at home and read

b) Go to work – it's a normal day

c) Visit family and friends and continue with the Christmas festivities

d) Light a bonfire and set off fireworks

99. When is New Year's Day celebrated in the UK?

a) 24th December

b) 26th December

c) 31st December

d) 1st January

100. What does Easter celebrate?

a) Crucifixion and subsequent Resurrection of Jesus Christ

b) The entry of Jesus Christ into Jerusalem seven days prior to the crucifixion

c) The birth of Jesus Christ

d) The start of the summer

101. What are Easter eggs made of?

a) They're real eggs

b) Real eggs covered in chocolate

c) Chocolate

d) Eggs covered in icing

102. The date of Easter changes each year but is always celebrated during at least one of two months. Which months?

    a) January or February

    b) March or April

    c) May or June

    d) July or August

103. When is St Valentine's Day?

    a) 5th November

    b) 31st December

    c) 1st January

    d) 14th February

104. Traditionally, what happens on St Valentine's Day?

    a) Bonfires are lit and fireworks set off

    b) A son cooks a special meal for his mother

    c) Lovers and husbands and wives generally exchange cards and gifts as a token of their love for one another

    d) Everyone has a day off work

105. What happens on Mothering Sunday?

  a) Children, both young and old, give their mother chocolates and flowers and try to make their day a nice one

  b) Everyone has a day off

  c) Mothers have to prepare a special meal for their children and invite them around for festivities

  d) Husbands have to prepare a meal for their wives and the wives in turn must finish the meal in its entirety

106. On which date does April Fool's Day fall?

  a) 30th April

  b) 20th April

  c) 10th April

  d) 1st April

107. What do people do on April Fool's Day?

  a) Exchange greetings cards and presents

  b) Invite family and friends around for food and drink

  c) Play practical jokes on each other (sometimes even newspapers and television stations try to fool their readers and viewers with a phoney story).

  d) Dress up and go trick or treating

108. When is Guy Fawkes Night?

    a) 5th November

    b) 31st December

    c) 1st January

    d) 14th February

109. What is celebrated on Guy Fawkes Night?

    a) New Year

    b) The birth of Jesus Christ

    c) The foiling of a plot in 1605 to blow up the then King of England and the Houses of Parliament

    d) The feast of St Guy Fawkes

110. Remembrance Day falls on 11th November each year. What is commemorated on this day?

    a) Those people from the UK who died in the Second World War

    b) Victims of the Bubonic Plague that hit the UK and Western Europe in the mid-14th century

    c) The people who died in both World Wars and later conflicts

    d) The Norman Conquest of Britain in 1066

111. Artificial versions of which flower are commonly worn on Remembrance Day?

    a) Daisies

    b) Poppies

    c) Daffodils

    d) Roses

112. **What do many Britons now do on Remembrance Day?**

    a) Light bonfires and set off fireworks

    b) Put on fancy dress outfits and go trick or treating

    c) Host a meal for family and friends

    d) Hold a two-minute silence

Questions Based on Chapter 4 in Appendix A

113. **General elections are held in Britain at least every how many years?**

    a) Five

    b) Four

    c) Six

    d) Three

114. **What does MP stand for?**

    a) Minister for police

    b) Master of parliament

    c) Member of parliament

    d) Minister of parliament

115. Who forms the Government?

   a) Military commanders

   b) The appointees of the Queen

   c) Senior politicians from all the main political parties

   d) MPs who belong to the largest political party in the House of Commons

116. There are two Houses of Parliament. One is the House of Commons. What is the other called?

   a) House of Cards

   b) House of Lords

   c) House of Wax

   d) House of Westminster

117. The PM is the leader of the political party in power. What does PM stand for?

   a) Powerful Man

   b) Prime Minister

   c) Powerful Minister

   d) Political manipulator

118. The PM lives at which famous address?

   a) 11 Downing Street

   b) Buckingham Palace

   c) Westminster Abbey

   d) 10 Downing Street

119. Who does the PM appoint and dismiss?

a) The Queen's or King's servants

b) The Queen or King

c) Ministers of State

d) MPs

120. Who sits in the Cabinet?

a) Ministers of State

b) The PM's political advisers

c) MPs

d) Civil servants

121. Margaret Thatcher resigned as PM in which year?

a) 1980

b) 1985

c) 1990

d) 1995

122. How many people sit in the Cabinet?

a) About 20

b) 2

c) 10

d) 40

123. How often does the Cabinet meet?

a) Every day

b) Once a week

c) Once a fortnight

d) Once a year

124. **Which minister is responsible for the UK economy?**

   a) The Governor of the Bank of England

   b) The PM

   c) The First Secretary to the Treasury

   d) The Chancellor of the Exchequer

125. **Which minister is responsible for immigration and law and order?**

   a) The PM

   b) The Chancellor of the Exchequer

   c) The Home Secretary

   d) The Foreign Secretary

126. **Decisions made in Cabinet are submitted to where for approval?**

   a) The Queen

   b) The Houses of Parliament

   c) The electorate

   d) To a television vote

127. **What type of constitution does the UK have?**

   a) A written Bill of Rights

   b) A very ancient one

   c) An unwritten one

   d) It doesn't have a constitution

128. Where are new laws passed?

  a) In Cabinet

  b) In the Courts

  c) By the Queen

  d) In the Houses of Parliament

129. In the UK, the job of the Courts is to do what?

  a) Interpret laws passed in the Houses of Parliament

  b) Pass laws

  c) Sentence criminals

  d) Overrule politicians

130. Name the three main political parties in the UK.

  a) Republicans, Democrats, and Independents

  b) Nationalists, Republicans, and Liberals

  c) Conservatives, Labour, and Liberal Democrats

  d) Conservatives, Liberals, and Nationalists

131. The second largest party in the House of Commons is officially called?

  a) The Losers

  b) The Nearly Men

  c) The Opposition

  d) Her Majesty's Loyal Opposition

132. What is the Shadow Cabinet?

a) Senior members of the second biggest party in Parliament who shadow government ministers in different government departments

b) Senior members of the biggest party in Parliament who aren't quite important enough to sit in the real Cabinet

c) Very senior members of the full Cabinet who are asked to remain behind after meeting to discuss policy with the PM

d) A meeting of the Cabinet which takes place at night

133. When are by-elections held?

a) Half-way through the life of a Parliament

b) Every two years

c) When an MP dies or resigns

d) Whenever the Government wants

134. Who opens Parliament?

a) The PM

b) The reigning monarch

c) A well-known celebrity

d) The Chancellor of the Exchequer

135. What happens during Question Time?

    a) MPs get to ask questions of government ministers

    b) The Speaker of the House of Commons is asked questions

    c) The Lord Chancellor is asked questions by members of the House of Lords

    d) The public get to ask questions of the PM and senior government ministers

136. What is the official title of the written record of proceedings in the Houses of Parliament called?

    a) *Hanson*

    b) *Hansard*

    c) *The Sun*

    d) *Today in Parliament*

137. Why is the UK said to have a 'free press'?

    a) There is no charge for newspapers or television

    b) You are free to say anything you want in the media

    c) It is free from government interference

    d) It is free of any original thoughts

138. **In practice what does the legal requirement for reporting of politics to be 'balanced' actually mean?**

   a) Giving equal time to rival viewpoints

   b) Asking tough questions of all politicians

   c) Giving free airtime to all political parties

   d) Allowing politicians to say what they want without questions

139. **What is the nickname for non-departmental public bodies?**

   a) The NHS

   b) The Civil Service

   c) NGOs

   d) Quangos

140. **The powers of the monarch are limited by what?**

   a) The army

   b) The powers of the monarch are unlimited

   c) The PM

   d) Constitutional law and convention

141. **In the UK, what must the reigning monarch always do?**

   a) Follow the advice of the PM on matters of government

   b) Give television interviews when asked

   c) Live in Buckingham Palace at weekends

   d) Attend Parliament when asked

142. **Queen Elizabeth the Second has reigned since what year?**

    a) 1952

    b) 1977

    c) 2002

    d) 1932

143. **The official title of the heir to the throne is?**

    a) The Prince of Tides

    b) The Prince of Wales

    c) The artist formerly known as Prince

    d) The Prince of Britain

144. **When is the Queen's Speech made?**

    a) At Christmas on television

    b) At the beginning of a new session of Parliament

    c) At the opening ceremony of the Commonwealth Games

    d) To the PM during her weekly audience

145. **What can the House of Lords do when presented with new laws from the House of Commons?**

    a) Throw them out and make new laws in its own right

    b) Tell the PM and the Queen what to do

    c) Sack MPs

    d) Delay the passage of the new laws but not overturn the new laws

146. **How many parliamentary constituencies are there throughout the UK?**

    a) 100

    b) 650

    c) 645

    d) 745

147. **What is the job of parliamentary committees?**

    a) To spend hours debating political issues

    b) To scrutinise legislation and investigate administration

    c) To question ministers and the PM

    d) To draw up new laws

148. **How can you get to see parliamentary debates?**

    a) On big screens in Trafalgar Square

    b) You're not allowed to attend parliamentary debates

    c) By taking a seat in the public galleries either through tickets or queuing at the public entrance

    d) Download a video podcast

149. **Who appoints or elects the Speaker of the House of Commons?**

    a) Directly elected by the public

    b) Appointed by the Queen on the advice of the PM

    c) Elected through a ballot of members of the biggest political party in the Commons

    d) Elected through a ballot of all MPs

150. What is the job of the Whips in Parliament?

a) To ensure that all MPs are sober and behave properly

b) To prevent members of the public from entering the Commons chamber

c) To gather gossip for their party leaders

d) Appointed by party leaders to ensure discipline and attendance of MPs at votes in the House of Commons

151. What recently happened to the role of hereditary life peers in the House of Lords?

a) They were all sacked

b) They had their automatic right to attend the House of Lords removed

c) They were barred from ever coming to the House of Lords again

d) They had their number expanded and some were given prominent government jobs

152. Who appoints life peers?

a) The PM

b) The Queen

c) They are self-appointed

d) The electorate

153. **What does the 'first past the post' electoral system mean in practice?**

   a) The candidate with the majority of votes is elected

   b) If there is no one candidate with a majority of vote the election is rerun

   c) Whichever party polls the most votes throughout the country has all their candidates elected

   d) The candidate with the most votes is elected

154. **What does a political party need to form a government?**

   a) To have polled the largest number of votes at a general election

   b) To have gained a majority of seats in the House of Commons

   c) To have gained a majority of seats in the House of Commons and the House of Lords

   d) The approval of the Queen

155. **Why do the two main UK political parties not support proportional representation for elections to the House of Commons?**

   a) They think it is unfair

   b) They believe it will lead to a one-party state

   c) They think it is too complex for the public to understand

   d) They believe it will lead to coalition government and instability

156. **What is the system used for elections to the Scottish Parliament and the Welsh and Northern Ireland Assemblies?**

    a) First past the post

    b) Whichever party polls the most votes wins the election

    c) Proportional representation

    d) The public votes for their favourite party but not individual candidates

157. **Why is it reckoned that membership of political parties has been falling in the UK during recent years?**

    a) Due to greater consensus between the parties on the main questions of economic management and social policy

    b) Because party membership has become very expensive

    c) Because parties can't afford to advertise for new members

    d) Because people have become more involved with pressure groups instead

158. **What tends to happen at Party Conferences?**

    a) Party members get to vote on who should represent the party at election time

    b) The policy of the party is debated by the membership

    c) The leader of the party stands for re-election

    d) New members are welcomed to the party

159. What is a pressure group?

    a) MPs who are not aligned to a political party

    b) A commercial, financial, industrial, trade, or professional organisation

    c) A committee of MPs whose job it is to quiz leading civil servants to check that they are doing a good job

    d) An organisation that tries to influence government policy, either directly or indirectly

160. What happens if the judiciary declares that a law passed by Parliament contravenes human rights?

    a) They are ignored – Parliament has the final say on the law

    b) The ruling automatically goes to the appeal court for further clarification

    c) The judge is sacked by the government

    d) The law has to be changed

161. Who appoints judges?

    a) The Queen

    b) The Prime Minister

    c) A panel of other judges

    d) The Lord Chancellor

162. Where are the headquarters of the Metropolitan Police?

    a) New Scotland Yard

    b) 221B Baker Street, London

    c) The Old Bailey, London

    d) The Royal Courts of Justice

163. **What does police 'operational independence' mean?**

   a) The government cannot instruct the police to arrest or proceed against any individual

   b) Members of the police force are immune from prosecution in the courts

   c) The police do not have to follow what they are told to do by the courts

   d) The police can arrest and imprison who they wish, when they want, for as long as they want

164. **What is the job of the civil service?**

   a) Cover up government errors

   b) Ensure government policy is carried out

   c) Ensure government policy is seen in a favourable light in the media

   d) Remain independent of the government at all times

165. **What happens to the civil service if at a general election the party in power changes?**

   a) Top civil servants are replaced by members of the new ruling party

   b) The civil service stops work and waits to be told what to do next

   c) They serve the new government loyally, looking to enact its policies

   d) They pick and choose which of the new Government's policies they wish to enact

166. **Large towns and cities in the UK tend to be administered by what?**

   a) An elected mayor

   b) The civil service in Whitehall

   c) A parish council

   d) A single authority such as a borough, metropolitan district, or city council

167. **What can happen if local authorities fail to deliver 'mandatory services'?**

   a) The head of the local authority can be sacked by central government

   b) The head of the local authority can be prosecuted through the courts by the police

   c) An election is held

   d) Citizens can take them to court

168. **Where does most of the money for local government come from?**

   a) The national lottery

   b) Council tax

   c) Central government funds

   d) A local income tax

169. **In which month are elections for local government held each year?**

   a) March

   b) April

   c) May

   d) June

170. **Wales and Scotland enjoy devolved government. What political issues are these institutions not allowed to make law on?**

    a) Health, education, and housing

    b) Pensions, legal affairs, and sport

    c) Social security, the environment, and rural affairs

    d) Defence, foreign affairs, and taxation

171. **In which city is the National Assembly for Wales based?**

    a) Cardiff

    b) Swansea

    c) Wrexham

    c) London

172. **How many members of the National Assembly for Wales are there, and how frequently are elections held?**

    a) 60 members, elections every five years

    b) 60 members, elections every four years

    c) 50 members, elections every five years

    d) 50 members, elections every four years

173. **In which city is the Scottish Parliament based?**

    a) Dundee

    b) Glasgow

    c) Edinburgh

    d) Aberdeen

174. How is the Scottish Parliament funded?

a) VAT on the sale of all goods in Scotland

b) The proceeds of all national lottery tickets sold in Scotland

c) Council tax

d) A grant from the UK government

175. In which building does the Northern Ireland Assembly meet?

a) Stormont

b) Windsor Park

c) The Europa, Belfast

d) Belfast City Hall

176. In which year was the Good Friday agreement signed?

a) 2000

b) 1999

c) 1998

d) 1986

177. In which year was the Council of Europe created?

a) 1949

b) 1945

c) 1973

d) 1956

178. **The UK's entry into the European Union was vetoed by France on how many occasions?**

   a) Once

   b) Never

   c) Twice

   d) Three times

179. **In which year did Britain join the European Union?**

   a) 1945

   b) 1949

   c) 1956

   d) 1973

180. **What is the main stated aim of the European Union?**

   a) For member states to become a single market

   b) The creation of a United States of Europe

   c) To have a military machine more powerful than America's

   d) To ensure the Eurovision song contest is broadcast in each member state

181. **What special rights do citizens of EU states have?**

   a) Freedom from arrest while travelling in other member states

   b) The right to travel to any EU country as long as they have a valid passport

   c) The right to claim state benefits while living in other member states

   d) The right to citizenship of all EU member states

182. **Where is the European Commission based?**

   a) Paris

   b) Brussels

   c) Strasbourg

   d) Berlin

183. **How frequently are elections to the European Parliament held?**

   a) Every four years

   b) Every five years

   c) Every six years

   d) Every seven years

184. **What powers does the European Parliament have?**

   a) The power to order the arrest of any citizen in any EU member state

   b) The power to impose taxes on the people of the UK

   c) The power to propose new laws for consideration by the council of ministers

   d) The power to scrutinise and debate the proposals and expenditure of the European Commission

185. **What is an EU regulation?**

   a) A proposal to member states that they should change their own law

   b) A law change that must be introduced by member states within a set time

   c) Specific rules which automatically have the force of law in all EU countries

   d) Laws which apply to all members states and if broken can lead to arrest and imprisonment

186. **How many states are there in the Commonwealth?**

   a) 184

   b) 104

   c) 84

   d) 53

187. **What are the key aims of the Commonwealth?**

   a) To develop democracy, eradicate poverty, and promote good government

   b) To become an economic and military rival to the United States

   c) To develop health programmes and deliver aid to starving people

   d) To ensure that the political and economic interests of the UK are furthered

188. **What are the key aims of the United Nations?**

   a) To develop health programmes and deliver aid to starving people

   b) To develop democracy, eradicate poverty, and promote good government

   c) To promote free trade

   d) To prevent war and maintain international peace and security

189. **The UK is a permanent member of the UN Security Council. What are the key aims of the council?**

   a) To promote free trade

   b) To recommend UN action in the event of international crisis and threats to peace

   c) To track down and capture wanted criminals from around the globe

   d) To ensure that there is no proliferation of nuclear weapons technology

190. **In which year was the present voting age of 18 set?**

    a) 1919

    b) 1929

    c) 1969

    d) 1989

191. **In order to vote in an election you must:**

    a) Be on the electoral register

    b) Be of sound mind and good character

    c) Own property

    d) Hold a British passport

192. **What is the deadline for return of electoral register forms?**

    a) 15th March

    b) 15th May

    c) 15th August

    d) 15th October

193. **Where is the electoral register held?**

    a) The Houses of Parliament

    b) Westminster Abbey

    c) Local electoral registration office or library

    d) Local registry office

194. **Citizens of the EU, resident in the UK, have the right to vote in which of the following?**

   a) Elections to the EU Parliament but no other elections

   b) All elections except national parliamentary elections

   c) Local council elections only

   d) No elections. They have to return to their home country to vote

195. **Citizens of the UK, Commonwealth, and which other country can vote in all public elections?**

   a) United States

   b) France

   c) Ireland

   d) Spain

196. **What age do you have to be before you can stand for election to public office?**

   a) 18

   b) 21

   c) 30

   d) 40

197. **What percentage of the vote must a candidate receive at an election to receive their deposit back?**

   a) 5 per cent

   b) 10 per cent

   c) 15 per cent

   d) 20 per cent

198. **You have to pay a deposit to stand for the UK Parliament, Scottish Parliament, or Welsh Assembly. How much is this deposit?**

    a) £500

    b) £5,000

    c) £50,000

    d) £500,000

199. **What deposit do you have to pay to stand as a candidate for the European Parliament?**

    a) £500

    b) £5,000

    c) £50,000

    d) £500,000

200. **Where can you find details of your local MP?**

    a) Local newspaper advert

    b) Teletext

    c) Phone book, *Yellow Pages,* and local library

    d) The UK Parliament Web site

201. **When MPs hold a 'surgery', what are they doing?**

    a) Performing dental work on patients to supplement their salary

    b) Speaking at a public meeting

    c) Going out and knocking on the door of the electorate

    d) Allowing constituents to call in person to their office to raise matters of concern

Answers

Here are the answers to those questions. Check below to see how you did.

Answers to the Questions Based on Chapter 2 in Appendix A

1. c		**18.** c
2. d		**19.** b
3. a		**20.** d
4. b		**21.** a
5. c		**22.** c
6. a		**23.** c
7. b		**24.** b
8. b		**25.** c
9. a		**26.** b
10. b		**27.** a
11. c		**28.** b
12. a		**29.** d
13. c		**30.** d
14. a		**31.** b
15. c		**32.** c
16. d		**33.** d
17. b		**34.** c

35. c	**39.** b
36. b	**40.** d
37. a	**41.** c
38. d	

Answers to the Questions Based on Chapter 3 in Appendix A

42. b	**57.** c
43. d	**58.** a
44. a	**59.** a
45. c	**60.** d
46. b	**61.** c
47. b	**62.** b
48. a	**63.** a
49. d	**64.** a
50. a	**65.** b
51. d	**66.** d
52. c	**67.** d
53. c	**68.** a
54. c	**69.** b
55. a	**70.** c
56. b	**71.** a

72. d	**93.** a
73. a	**94.** c
74. b	**95.** d
75. c	**96.** d
76. a	**97.** b
77. a	**98.** c
78. c	**99.** d
79. a	**100.** a
80. c	**101.** c
81. a	**102.** b
82. b	**103.** d
83. d	**104.** c
84. a	**105.** a
85. c	**106.** d
86. d	**107.** c
87. b	**108.** a
88. c	**109.** c
89. a	**110.** c
90. c	**111.** b
91. d	**112.** d
92. a	

Answers to the Questions Based on Chapter 4 in Appendix A

113. a		**134.** b	
114. c		**135.** a	
115. d		**136.** b	
116. b		**137.** c	
117. b		**138.** a	
118. d		**139.** d	
119. c		**140.** d	
120. a		**141.** a	
121. c		**142.** a	
122. a		**143.** b	
123. b		**144.** b	
124. d		**145.** d	
125. c		**146.** c	
126. b		**147.** b	
127. c		**148.** c	
128. d		**149.** d	
129. a		**150.** d	
130. c		**151.** b	
131. d		**152.** a	
132. a		**153.** d	
133. c		**154.** b	

155. d	**179.** d
156. c	**180.** a
157. a	**181.** b
158. b	**182.** b
159. d	**183.** b
160. d	**184.** d
161. d	**185.** c
162. a	**186.** d
163. a	**187.** a
164. b	**188.** d
165. c	**189.** b
166. d	**190.** c
167. d	**191.** a
168. c	**192.** d
169. c	**193.** c
170. d	**194.** b
171. a	**195.** c
172. b	**196.** b
173. c	**197.** a
174. d	**198.** a
175. a	**199.** b
176. c	**200.** c
177. a	**201.** d
178. c	

Index

• **F** •

Notes

Notes

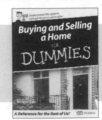

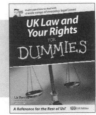

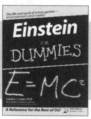